Black Classics

The
SOUL OF A WOMAN

Published by
THE X PRESS, 55 BROADWAY MARKET, LONDON E8 4PH.
TEL: 0171 729 1199 FAX: 0171 729 1771
E-MAIL: Xpress @ maxis.co.uk

© The X Press 1996.

Distributed by Turnaround, 27 Horsell Road, London N5 1XL
Tel: 0171 609 7836

Printed by BPC Paperbacks Ltd, Aylesbury, Bucks.
ISBN 1-874509-39-5

Introduction

The Black woman as novelist is a powerful and exciting force in contemporary fiction. Ever since Maya Angelou revealed why 'the caged bird sings' and Alice Walker took our minds deep into the 'colour purple', everybody's wanted to be a 'sista'. Because Black women are the prism through which the searing rays of race, class and sex are first focused and then refracted. So when Terry McMillan tells it like it is about how Stella got her groove back, she's telling us of her life and not only of her life but of our lives too.

The Soul of A Woman stretches the full range of the emotions and experiences and is nothing if not constantly 'edutaining'.

Share with us the pleasure of enjoying the forgotten talents of many of black writing's greatest names:

Grace W. Tompkins.
Little is known about Grace Tompkins' life and literary career other than the little which was written about her in the 'contributors' notes' of the 'Negro Story' magazine to which she regularly contributed in the forties.

Zora Neale Hurston (1901-60), most famous for having penned the bestseller *Their Eyes Were Watching God*, often cited as inspiring Alice Walker's *The Color Purple*.

Ruth D. Todd was a full time servant and part time short story writer for the 'Colored American Magazine' in its heyday in the twenties. She was born in 1878, but there is no information as to what happenedto her after the magazine folded.

Jessie Fauset (1882-1961) was born in New Jersey of middle class parents, and grew up in Philadelphia. As part of the Harlem Rennaissance of writers (which included Langston Hughes and Zora Neale Hurston), she achieved much success with her four published novels: *There is Confusion* (1924), *Plum Bun* (1929), *Chinaberry Tree* (1931) and *Comedy: American Style* (1933).

Frances E. W. Harper (1825-1911). Born a free slave in Maryland, USA, Harper went on to write the hugely popular *Iola* (X Press

Classics), reputedly the most popular book of fiction by a black person in the nineteenth century.

Victoria Earle (1861-1907) was born into slavery but was able to attend school whilst working as a domestic. As an adult she was devoted to the promotion of civil and social rights for black women.

Angelina Weld Grimke (1880-1958) grew up in Boston in a life of relative privilege. Her father was executive director of the National Association for the Advancement of Colored People and Grimke herself went on to teach at Dunbar High School. The majority of her short stories and essays were published in the black literary magazines, 'The Crisis' and 'Opportunity'.

Alice Dunbar-Nelson (1875-1935) was born in New Orleans, a city which forms the backdrop to much of her fiction. Her celebrated collection, *The Goodness of St Roque*, (1898) was the first collection of short stories to be published by an African-American woman.

Pauline Elizabeth Hopkins was born in Portland, Maine in 1859. Much of her early fiction was published in the 'Colored American Magazine' where she later became literary editor. Her novel *A Love Supreme* (X Press Classics) was her best known work and the only one published in book form during her lifetime.

Dorothy West grew up in Boston and won her first literary competition with her story, 'The Typewriter' at the age of eighteen. She founded 'New Challenge' magazine with Richard Wright in 1937 and is the author of *The Living is Easy* (1948), an excetpional and memorable work of fiction

Gwendolyn Bennett (1902-1981) was born in Giddings, Texas. She was one of the founders and contributors to the Harlem Renaissance journal, 'Fire!' where her only short story, 'Wedding Day' was published.

Nella Larsen (1891-1964) was born in Chicago and initially trained and worked as a nurse before moving to New York. In 1929 her novel, *Quicksand* won the bronze medal from the Harmon Foundation. She was also the first black woman to receive an award from the Guggenheim Fellowship.

Melissa Linn's 'All That Hair' is believed to be the only piece of fiction she ever had published and won the Writer's Digest Contest , sponsored by 'Negro Story' magazine. She was born in Marietta, Ohio, but little else is known about her.

Sylvia Dubois was born into slavery, though her exact birth date is unknown. In *The Slave Who Whipped Her Mistress and Gained Her Freedom* Dubois recalls her own life as a slave and her eventual freedom. When her reminiscences were originally printed in 1883, Dubois was reputedly over 100 years old.

Justice Wears Dark Glasses

by
GRACE W. TOMPKINS

THE GRAY-HAIRED MAN had a kind face, thought Mamie. He would believe her. He removed his glasses and slowly polished them as she nervously shifted from one foot to the other. The big man's hold on her arm tightened as she cleared her throat in an attempt to speak. Carefully replacing his glasses, the man behind the desk spoke,

"Yes, Spraggins?"

"Another one, sir. Stole two dresses."

"I—I—" Mamie's voice died away.

"What are you trying to say?" The man's voice was gentle.

"Mister, I never stole anything. Just wanted to try on the dresses. That's all. . . "

"Salesgirl saw her duck, sir, caught her with them. Here they are." Spraggins laid the dresses on the desk.

"Yes, sir. I mean, no . . ." Mamie's voice mounted to a wail.

"She wouldn't let me try them on. I asked her, and she . . ."

The gray-haired man held up his hand for silence. He pushed one button in the long row that edged the glass-topped desk. Then he began to write rapidly on a pad of paper. A young woman came in. He detached the sheet and handed it to her, and she left.

An agonizing twitch had set up in Mamie's stomach. She scratched her head nervously and shifted her weight again. The silence only increased her terror. Spraggins cleared his throat, and the sound echoed like a shot in the room.

The man at the desk had not once looked in her direction. She stared hard, trying to catch his eye. You know I didn't steal them, she

1

thought. You're just trying to scare me. She didn't want to wait on me. I didn't steal . . . you know I didn't steal . . . she didn't want to wait to me . . . The sentences chased each other around and around in Mamie's mind, but her throat was dry, and not a word came out.

The office door opened, and the young woman returned with two more. Mamie recognized the salesgirl, but she had never seen the other one.

"Miss Donovan, did you see this theft?"

"Yes, Mr. Feldman."

Mamie was bewildered, for the reply had come from the strange woman.

"And you, too?" He turned to the salesgirl.

"Yes, sir." Her reply was hardly audible, and she reddened.

Mamie found her voice: "No, no . . . You said I had to ask the floorwalker, and when I tried to talk to him, this man brought me up here!"

"A likely story!" The man behind the desk no longer looked kind and gentle. "You're not only a thief but a liar too. Here are three witnesses who saw you take them. We're going to teach you . . . you folks to stay out of Manson's, and there's just one way to do it!"

He nodded to Spraggans, who immediately caught Mamie by the arm and started for the door. She struggled. "What are you going to do? What—" Her voice ended in a cry as a vicious upward jerk of her bent arm put an abrupt end to the struggle.

They went down in the freight elevator and out the side door to the rotunda. The blue of the patrol wagon made her wonder who was being arrested. And then she was hustled unceremoniously between two big rough policemen, and the grilled door was slammed shut.

The flies buzzing around a spittoon held Mamie's eyes as she plucked and twisted a corner of her jacket. The mumbled words of the bondsman were lost in the roar of the blood pounding in her ears. A colored policeman stopped to talk to the bondsman. A hopeful gleam lighted Mamie's pain-dulled eyes, but died quickly as the man laughed and sauntered away. After a long wait, she was free to go home until Monday morning. The bondsman had her lone ten dollar bill in his pocket.

On reaching the street, she found that she did not have carfare. It was a long way to 33rd Street, but she did not have the courage to ask anyone for eight cents. After the first ten blocks she walked in a pain-ridden daze. Passersby thought she was drunk. A man flung a coarse remark at her.

Lena saw her coming and ran down the rickety steps to meet her.

"Mamie! You're sick!"

"I've been arrested."

"Arrested? Jesus!"

Lena helped her into the stuffy bedroom and began taking her street things off. She finally got her to sleep.

Mamie awoke refreshed. Then she remembered, I have to go to court Monday. They arrested me for stealing. I had better get a lawyer, but I haven't any money. She had a strange empty kind of feeling. Lena came in.

"Get dressed," she said. "We're going to see Mr. Clark."

"I ain't got no money to get no lawyer."

"He'll take it in payments. You can't let 'em get away with this."

"They can't do nothin'. I didn't steal them dresses."

"They had you arrested, didn't they? It's a lousy frame! They framed you 'cause they don't want colored people in their damn store. It shoulda been me! You just ain't no fighter!"

"What could I do? The big man grabbed me before you could say 'scat,' and the boss man thought I was lying. Both them women lied. I never even seen the big one with the yellow hair."

"It's a lousy frame. A damn lousy frame!" said Lena.

Mr. Clark was both ponderous and suave. Much of what he said was so veiled in legal terminology that it went over Mamie's head.

"Of course Illinois has a civil rights law under which you may sue when exonerated. Now if you sue for punitive damages the court may award you a dollar. What the hell? It won't pay back what you lose. AND . . . you could go right back in the store again tomorrow and the same thing might happen again. Now if you sue to obtain revocation of license, you won't get to first base. And of course that's all based on your being exonerated."

Mamie looked perplexed.

"Now if they find you guilty—"

"But I ain't," she interrupted him.

"I know, I know." His voice was soothing. "But the law's a funny thing. If those women and the store detective testify under oath that they saw you, then it's your word against three. Of course we can produce character witnesses. Now if you'll . . ."

3

Court was crowded. Mamie's case was near the end of the docket. Her lawyer sat importantly inside the railing with half a dozen others. She listened carefully to each case, to the testimony of witnesses, to the pleas of the attorneys. Lena patted her hand reassuringly. After six cases in a row had been dismissed for lack of sufficient evidence, she took heart and relaxed a little.

"Manson versus Mamie Jones, shoplifting. Mamie Jones!"

Mamie got to her feet trembling and walked through the enclosure.

As she looked in the face of the judge, her fear left her. To her right stood Spraggins, the two women, and another elderly man, counsel for the store. Her pastor and her doctor had joined her lawyer on the left. Lena stood directly behind her with a protective hand resting on her shoulder. The judge was white haired, and his seamed face was calm. There was an amused twinkle in his eyes as he looked at her, and she almost smiled at him.

Her fear gone, she told her story in a clear steady voice. The judge nodded sympathetically several times as she talked. Then the strange blond woman was talking. She said that she had watched Mamie paw through the dresses on the counter, walk around a bit, and return to the counter. Mamie had taken two dresses and started away.

"Did you say anything to her?" asked the judge.

"No. I thought she was going to approach a salesgirl and try the dresses on."

"Then what happened?"

"She looked around in a furtive sort of way and then started in the direction of the ladies' washroom."

"No . . . I don't even know where the washroom—" began Mamie.

"Please," said the judge.

"A salesgirl accosted her," continued the woman, "and she broke into a run. Mr. Spraggins caught her."

Mamie stared fascinated at the woman as she talked clearly with every evidence of telling the truth. The salesgirl corroborated every word. Spraggins said he had seen the commotion and had arrived in time to see Mamie drop the dresses to the floor.

As Mr. Clark began to talk, Mamie felt a surge of relief. "Your Honor, this woman had no need to steal. She entered the store in good faith with a ten-dollar bill to buy two of the dresses advertised at $3.99 in the basement sale. She was treated with discourtesy, denied the privilege of trying on her selection, roughly handled by the store detective and the floor walker, and called a liar and a thief by the manager. This woman is respectable. Her reputation is unimpeachable, as these three witnesses will affirm. It is quite obvious that Manson's is trying to intimidate the Negroes who insist upon trading in the store when their publicized policy is not to wait upon colored people."

The last statement brought a quick reprimand and a warning from the judge. He waived the testimony of the character witnesses, and Mamie felt satisfied that she had won.

The lawyer for Manson's was speaking:

"For the past six months, there has been a wave of petty thieving in the store. Women's apparel sections are the hardest hit. We have got to stop it. This woman was caught red-handed. Probably inexperience made her unsuccessful in making away with the merchandise without detection. But the fact remains that three people say the attempt was made. Manson must make an example of her and deter the others with whom she may be associated."

The judge was nodding sympathetically. He turned inquiringly toward Mr. Clark, but the lawyer had nothing to add. The court was very quiet. Mamie was sure every one could hear the pounding of her heart against her ribs. Then the judge began to speak, and his voice was low and friendly:

"I do not believe you are an habitual thief. You work. That is to your credit. Your friends are here in defense of your character as they know it. That is also in your favor. The morale of their working staff must be preserved. I cannot believe that three witnesses have lied under oath. In view of the facts as presented, I have no alternative but to find you guilty and sentence you to thirty days in jail."

In the anteroom, Abe Clark was saying, "My fee is thirty-five dollars. I have a note here for the amount. Will you sign it, please?"

Mamie signed.

The Gilded Six Bits

by
<u>ZORA NEALE HURSTON</u>

IT WAS A NEGRO YARD around a Negro house in a Negro settlement that looked to the payroll of the G. and G. Fertilizer Works for its support.

But there was something happy about the place. The front yard was parted in the middle by a sidewalk from gate to doorstep a sidewalk edged on either side by quart bottles driven neck down into the ground on a slant. A mess of homey flowers planted without a plan but blooming cheerily from their helter-skelter places. The fence and the house were whitewashed. The porch and steps scrubbed white.

The front door stood open to the sunshine so that the floor of the front room could finish drying after its weekly scouring. It was Saturday. Everything clean from the front gate to the privy house. Yard raked so that the strokes of the rake would make a pattern. Fresh newspaper cut in fancy edge on the kitchen shelves

Missie May was bathing herself in the galvanized washtub in the bedroom. Her dark-brown skin glistened under the soapsuds that skittered down from her washrag. Her stiff young breasts thrust forward aggressively like broad-based cones with the tips lacquered in black.

She heard men's voices in the distance and glanced at the dollar clock on the dresser

"Humph! I'm way behind time t'day! Joe's going to be here 'fore I git my clothes on if I don't make haste."

She grabbed the clean meal sack at hand and dried herself hurriedly and began to dress. But before she could tie her slippers, there came the ring of singing metal on wood Nine times.

Missie May grinned with delight. She had not seen the big, tall man come stealing in the gate and creep up the walk grinning happily at the joyful mischief he was about to commit. But she knew that it was her husband throwing silver dollars in the door for her to pick up and pile beside her plate at dinner. It was this way every Saturday afternoon. The nine dollars hurled into the open door, he scurried to a hiding place behind the cape jasmine bush and waited.

Missie May promptly appeared at the door in mock alarm.

"Who dat chunkin' money in my doorway?" she demanded. No answer from the yard. She leaped off the porch and began to search the shrubbery. She peeped under the porch and hung over the gate to look up and down the road. While she did this, the man behind the jasmine darted to the chinaberry tree. She spied him and gave chase.

"Nobody ain't gonna be chuckin' money at me and I not do 'em nothin'," she shouted in mock anger. He ran around the house with Missie May at his heels. She overtook him at the kitchen door. He ran inside but could not close it after him before she crowded in and locked with him in a rough and tumble. For several minutes the two were a furious mass of male and female energy. Shouting, laughing, twisting, turning, tussling, tickling each other in the ribs; Missie May clutching onto Joe and Joe trying, but not too hard, to get away.

"Missie May, take your hand out my pocket! Joe shouted out between laughs.

"I ain't, Joe, not lessen you gwine gimme whatever it is you got in your pocket. Turn it go, Joe, do I'll tear your clothes."

"Go on tear 'em. You de one dat pushes de needles round here. Move your hand, Missie May."

"Lemme git dat paper sack out your pocket. I bet it's candy kisses."

"Tain't. Move your hand. Woman ain't got no business in a man's clothes nohow. Go way."

Missie May gouged way down and gave an upward jerk and triumphed.

"Unhhunh! I got it. It 'tis so candy kisses. I knowed you had somethin' for me in your clothes. Now I got to see what's in every pocket you got."

Joe smiled indulgently and let his wife go through all of his pockets and take out the things that he had hidden there for her to find. She bore off the chewing gum, the cake of sweet soap, the pocket handkerchief as if she had wrested them from him, as if they had not been bought for the sake of this friendly battle.

"Whew! Dat play-fight done got me all warmed up," Joe

exclaimed. "Got me some water in de kettle?"

"Your water is on de fire and your clean things is cross de bed. Hurry up and wash yourself and git changed so we can eat. I'm hungry." As Missie said this, she bore the steaming kettle into the bedroom.

"You ain't hungry, sugar," Joe contradicted her. "You're jes' a little empty. I'm de one what's hungry. I could eat up camp meetin', back off association, and drink Jordan dry. Have it on de table when I git out de tub."

"Don't you mess with my business, man. You git in your clothes. I'm a real wife, not no dress and breath. I might not look like one, but if you burn me, you won't git a thing but wife ashes."

Joe splashed in the bedroom, and Missie May fanned around in the kitchen. A fresh red and white checked cloth on the table. Big pitcher of buttermilk beaded with pale drops of butter from the churn. Hot fried mullet, crackling bread, ham hocks atop a mound of string beans and new potatoes, and perched on the windowsill, a pan of spicy potato pudding.

Very little talk during the meal, but that little consisted of banter that pretended to deny affection but in reality flaunted it. Like when Missie May reached for a second helping of the potato. Joe snatched it out of her reach.

After Missie May had made two or three unsuccessful grabs at the pan, she begged, "Aw, Joe, gimme some more of that potato."

"Nope, sweetenin' is for us men-folks. Y'all pretty lil frail eels don't need nothin' like dis. You too sweet already."

"Please, Joe."

"Naw, naw. I don't want you to git no sweeter than what you is already. We goin' down de road a lil piece tonight, so you go put on your Sunday-go-to-meetin' things." Missie May looked at her husband to see if he was playing some prank. "Sho nuff, Joe?"

"Yeah. We goin' to de ice-cream parlor."

"Where de ice-cream parlor at, Joe?"

"A new man done come here from Chicago and he done got a place and took and opened it up for a ice-cream parlor, and being as it's real swell, I wants you to be one of de first ladies to walk in there and have some set down."

"Do Jesus. I ain't knowed nothin' 'bout it. Who de man done it?"

"Mister Otis D. Slemmons, of spots and places—Memphis, Chicago, Jacksonville, Philadelphia, and so on."

"Dat heavy-set man with his mouth full of gold teethes?"

8

"Yeah. Where did you see him at?"

"I went down to de store to git a box of lye, and I seen him standing on de corner talkin' to some of de men, and I come on back and went to scrubbin' de floor, and he passed and tipped his hat whilst I was scourin' de steps. I thought I never seen *him* before."

Joe smiled pleasantly. "Yeah, he's up to date. He got de finest clothes I ever seen on a colored man's back."

"Aw, he don't look no better in his clothes than you do in yours. He got a gut on him, and he's so chuckleheaded, he got a bump behind his neck."

Joe looked down at his own abdomen and said wistfully: "Wish I had a build on me like he got. He ain't puzzlegutted, honey. He jes' got a corporation. Dat makes him look like a rich white man. All rich men have got some belly on 'em."

"I've seen de pictures of Henry Ford and he's a spare-built man, and Rockefeller look like he ain't got but one gut. But Ford and Rockefeller and dis Slemmons and all the rest can be as many-gutted as they please, I'm satisfied with you jes' like you is, baby. God took pattern after a pine tree and built you noble. You're a pretty man, and if I knowed any way to make you more pretty still, I'd take and do it.

Joe reached over gently and toyed with Missie May s ear. "You jes' say dat cause you love me, but I know I can't hold no light to Otis D. Slemmons. I ain't never been nowhere, and I ain't got nothin' but you."

Missie May got on his lap and kissed him and he kissed back in kind. Then he went on. "All de women is crazy 'bout him everywhere he go."

"How you know dat, Joe?"

"He told us so hisself."

"Dat don't make it so. His mouth is cut crossways, ain't it? Well, he can lie jes' like anybody else."

"Good Lord, Missie! You women sho is hard to sense into things. He's got a five-dollar gold piece for a stickpin, and he got a ten-dollar gold piece on his watch chain, and his mouth is jes' crammed full of gold teethes. Sho wish it was mine. And what make it so cool, he got money cumulated. And women give it all to him."

"I don't see what de women see in him. I wouldn't give him a wink if de sheriff was after him."

"Well, he told us how de white women in Chicago give him all dat gold money. So he don't 'low nobody to touch it at all. Not even put their finger on it. They told him not to. You can admire it, but don't

9

touch it."

"Why don't he stay up there where they're so crazy 'bout him?"

"I reckon they done made him vast-rich, and he wants to travel some. He says they wouldn't leave him hit a lick of work. He got more lady people crazy 'bout him than he can shake a stick at."

"Joe, I hates to see you so dumb. Dat stray nigger jes' tell y'all anything and y'all believe it."

"Go 'head on now, honey, and put on your clothes. He talking 'bout his pretty women—I want him to see mine. "

Missie May went off to dress, and Joe spent the time trying to make his stomach punch out like Slemmons's middle. He tried the rolling swagger of the stranger, but found that his tall bone-and-muscle stride fitted ill with it. He just had time to drop back into his seat before Missie May came in, dressed to go.

On the way home that night Joe was exultant. "Didn't I say ole Otis was swell? Cain't he talk Chicago talk? Wasn't dat funny what he said when great big fat ole Ida Armstrong come in? He asked me, 'Who is dat broad with de forte shake?' Dat's a new word. We always thought forty was a set of figures but he showed us where it means a whole heap of things. Sometimes he don't say forty, he jes' say thirty-eight and two, and dat mean de same thing. Know what he told me when I was paying for our ice cream? He say, 'I have to hand it to you, Joe. Dat wife of yours is jes' thirty-eight and two. Yessuh, she's forte!' Ain't he killin'?"

"He'll do in case of a rush. But he sho is got a heap of gold on him. Dat's de first time I ever seed gold money. It looked good on him sho nuff, but it'd look a whole heap better on you."

"Who, me? Missie May, you're crazy! Where would a potman like me git gold money from?"

Missie May was silent for a minute, then she said, "Us might find some goin' long de road sometime. Us could."

"Who would be losin' gold money round here? We ain't even seen none these white folks wearin' no gold money on their watch chain. You must be figuring' Mister Packard or Mister Cadillac goin' pass through here."

"You don't know what been lost 'round here. Maybe somebody way back in memorial times lost they gold money and went on off and it ain't never been found. And then if we was to find it, you could wear some without havin' no gang of women like dat Slemmons say he got."

Joe laughed and hugged her. "Don't be so wishful 'bout me. I'm satisfied de way I is. So long as I be your husband, I don't care 'bout nothin' else. I'd rather all de other women in de world to be dead than for you to have de toothache. Less we go to bed and git our night rest."

It was Saturday night once more before Joe could parade his wife in Slemmons's ice-cream parlor again. He worked the night shift, and Saturday was his only night off. Every other evening around six o'clock he left home, and dying dawn saw him hustling home around the lake, where the challenging sun flung a flaming sword from east to west across the trembling water.

That was the best part of life—going home to Missie May. Their whitewashed house, the mock battle on Saturday, the dinner and ice cream parlor afterward, church on Sunday nights, when Missie out-dressed any woman in town —all, everything, was right.

One night around eleven the acid ran out at the G. and G. The foreman knocked off the crew and let the steam die down. As Joe rounded the lake on his way home, a lean moon rode the lake in a silver boat. If anybody had asked Joe about the moon on the lake, he would have said he hadn't paid it any attention. But he saw it with his feelings. It made him yearn painfully for Missie. Creation obsessed him. He thought about children. They had been married more than a year now. They had money put away. They ought to be making little feet for shoes. A little boy-child would be about right.

He saw a dim light in the bedroom and decided to come in through the kitchen door. He could wash the fertilizer dust off himself before presenting himself to Missie May. It would be nice for her not to know that he was there until he slipped into his place in bed and hugged her back. She always liked that.

He eased the kitchen door open slowly and silently, but when he went to set his dinner bucket on the table, he bumped into a pile of dishes, and something crashed to the floor. He heard his wife gasp in fright and hurried to reassure her.

"It's me, honey. Don't git scared."

There was a quick, large movement in the bedroom. A rustle, a thud, and a stealthy silence. The light went out.

What? Robbers? Murderers? Some varmint attacking his helpless wife, perhaps. He struck a match, threw himself on guard, and stepped over the doorsill into the bedroom.

The great belt on the wheel of Time slipped and eternity stood still. By the match light he could see the man's legs fighting with his breeches in his frantic desire to get them on. He had both chance and

11

time to kill the intruder in his helpless condition—half in and half out of his pants—but he was too weak to take action. The shapeless enemies of humanity that live in the hours of Time had waylaid Joe He was assaulted in his weakness. Like Samson awakening after his haircut. So he just opened his mouth and laughed.

The match went out, and he struck another and lit the lamp. A howling wind raced across his heart, but underneath its fury he heard his wife sobbing and Slemmons pleading for his life. Offering to buy it with all that he had Please, suh, don't kill me. Sixty-two dollars at de store. Gold money."

Joe just stood. Slemmons looked at the window, but it was screened. Joe stood out like a rough-backed mountain between him and the door. Barring him from escape, from sunrise, from life.

He considered a surprise attack upon the big clown that stood there, grinning like a Cheshire cat. But before his fist could travel an inch, Joe's own rushed out to crush him like a battering ram. Then Joe stood over him.

"Git into your damn rags, Slemmons, and dat quick."

Slemmons scrambled to his feet and into his vest and coat. As he grabbed his hat, Joe in his fury overrode his intentions and grabbed at Slemmons with his left hand and struck at him with his right. The right landed. The left grazed the front of his vest. Slemmons was knocked a somersault into the kitchen and fled through the open door. Joe found himself alone with Missie May, with the golden watch charm clutched in his left fist. A short bit of broken chain dangled between his fingers.

Missie May was sobbing. Wails of weeping without words. Joe stood, and after a while he found out that he had something in his hand. And then he stood and felt without thinking and without seeing with his natural eyes. Missie May kept on crying and Joe kept on feeling so much; and not knowing what to do with all his feelings, he put Slemmons's watch charm in his pants pocket and took a good laugh and went to bed.

"Missie May, what you cryin' for?"

"Cause I love you so hard and I know you don't love me no more."

Joe sank his face into the pillow for a spell, then he said huskily. "You don't know de feelings of dat yet, Missie May."

"Oh Joe, honey, he said he was going to give me dat gold money, and he jes' kept on after me."

Joe was very still and silent for a long time. Then he said, "Well, don't cry no more, Missie May. I got your gold piece for you."

The hours went past on their rusty ankles. Joe still and quiet on one bed-rail and Missie May wrung dry of sobs on the other. Finally the sun's tide crept up on the shore of night and drowned all its hours. Missie May, with her face, stiff and streaked, towards the window saw the dawn come into her yard. It was day. Nothing more. Joe wouldn't be coming home as usual. No need to fling open the front door and sweep off the porch, making it nice for Joe. Never no more breakfasts to cook; no more washing and starching of Joe's jumper-jackets and pants. No more nothing. So why get up?

With this strange man in her bed, she felt embarrassed to get up and dress. She decided to wait till he had dressed and gone. Then she would get up, dress quickly, and be gone forever beyond reach of Joe's looks and laughs. But he never moved. Red light turned to yellow, then white.

From beyond the no-man's-land between them came a voice. A strange voice that yesterday had been Joe's.

"Missie May, ain't you gonna fix me no breakfast?"

She sprang out of bed. "Yeah, Joe. I didn't reckon you was hungry."

No need to die today. Joe needed her for a few more minutes anyhow.

Soon there was a roaring fire in the cookstove. Water bucket full and two chickens killed. Joe loved fried chicken and rice. She didn't deserve a thing and good Joe was letting her cook him some breakfast. She rushed hot biscuits to the table as Joe took his seat.

He ate with his eyes in his plate. No laughter, no banter.

Missie May, you ain't eatin' your breakfast."

"I don't choose none. I thank you."

His coffee cup was empty. She sprang to refill it. When she turned from the stove and bent to set the cup beside Joe s plate, she saw the yellow coin on the table between them.

She slumped into her seat and wept into her arms.

Presently Joe said calmly, "Missie May, you cry too much. Don't look back like Lot's wife and turn to salt."

The sun, the hero of every day, the impersonal old man that beams as brightly on death as on birth, came up every morning and raced across the blue dome and dipped into the sea of fire every evening. Water ran down hill and birds nested.

Missie knew why she didn't leave Joe. She couldn't. She loved him too much, but she could not understand why Joe didn't leave her. He was polite, even kind at times, but aloof.

There were no more Saturday romps. No ringing silver dollars to stack beside her plate. No pockets to rifle. In fact, the yellow coin in his trousers was like a monster hiding in the cave of his pockets to destroy her.

She often wondered if he still had it, but nothing could have induced her to ask nor yet to explore his pockets to see for herself. Its shadow was in the house whether or no.

One night Joe came home around midnight and complained of pains in the back. He asked Missie to rub him down with liniment. It had been three months since Missie had touched his body and it all seemed strange. But she rubbed him. Grateful for the chance. Before morning, youth triumphed and Missie exulted. But the next day, as she joyfully made up their bed, beneath her pillow she found the piece of money with the bit of chain attached.

Alone to herself, she looked at the thing with loathing, but look she must. She took it into her hands with trembling and saw first thing that it was no gold piece. It was a gilded half dollar. Then she knew why Slemmons had forbidden anyone to touch his gold. He trusted village eyes at a distance not to recognize his stickpin as a gilded quarter and his watch charm as a four-bit piece.

She was glad at first that Joe had left it there. Perhaps he was through with her punishment. They were man and wife again. Then another thought came dawning at her. He had come home to buy from her as if she were any woman in the long house. Fifty cents for her love. As if to say that he could pay as well as Slemmons. She slid the coin into his Sunday pants pocket and dressed herself and left his house.

Halfway between her house and the quarters she met her husband's mother, and after a short talk she turned and went back home. Never would she admit defeat to that woman, who prayed for it nightly. If she had not the substance of marriage, she had the outside show. Joe must leave her. She let him see she didn't want his old gold four-bits too.

She saw no more of the coin for some time, though she knew that Joe could not help finding it in his pocket. But his health kept poor, and he came home at least every ten days to be rubbed.

The sun swept around the horizon, trailing its robes of weeks and days. One morning as Joe came in from work, he found Missie May chopping wood. Without a word he took the ax and chopped a huge pile before he stopped.

14

"You ain't got no business choppin' wood, and you know it."

"How come? I been choppin' it for de last longest."

"I ain't blind. You makin' feet for shoes."

"Won't you be glad to have a li'l baby chile, Joe?"

"You know dat without asking me."

"It's gonna be a boy chile and de very spit of you."

"You reckon, Missie May?"

"Who else could it look like?"

Joe said nothing, but he thrust his hand deep into his pocket and fingered something there.

It was almost six months later Missie May took to bed, and Joe went and got his mother to come wait on the house.

Missie May was delivered of a fine boy. Her travail was over when Joe came in from work one morning. His mother and the old women were drinking great bowls of coffee around the fire in the kitchen.

The minute Joe came into the room, his mother called him aside.

"How did Missie May make out?" he asked quickly.

"Who, dat gal? She strong as a ox. She's gonna have plenty more. We done fixed her with de sugar and lard to sweeten her for de next one."

Joe stood silent awhile.

"You ain't asked 'bout de baby, Joe. You oughta be mighty proud cause he sho is de spittin' image of you, son. Dat's yours all right, if you never git another one, dat one is yours. And you know I'm mighty proud too, son, cause I never thought well of you marryin' Missie May cause her ma used to fan her foot round right smart, and I been mighty scared dat Missie May was gonna git misput on her road."

Joe said nothing. He fooled around the house till late in the day, then, just before he went to work, he went and stood at the foot of the bed and asked his wife how she felt. He did this every day during the week.

On Saturday he went to Orlando to make his market. It had been a long time since he had done that.

Meat and lard, meal and flour, soap and starch. Cans of corn and tomatoes. All the staples. He fooled around town for a while and bought bananas and apples. Way after a while he went around to the candy store.

"Hello, Joe," the clerk greeted him. "Ain't seen you in a long time."

"Nope, I ain't been here. Been round in spots and places."

"Want some of them molasses kisses you always buy?"

"Yessuh." He threw the gilded half dollar on the counter. "Will dat spend?"

"What is it, Joe? Well, I'll be doggone! A goldplated four-bit piece. Where'd you git it, Joe?"

"Off of a stray nigger dat come through Eatonville. He had it on his watch chain for a charm—goin' round making out it's gold money. Ha ha! He had a quarter on his tie pin, and it was all golded up too. Tryin' to fool people. Makin' out he so rich and everything. Ha! Ha! Tryin' to steal off folk's wives from home."

"How did you git it, Joe? Did he fool you, too?"

"Who, me? Naw suh! He ain't fooled me none. Know what I done? He come round me with his smart talk. I hauled off and knocked him down and took his old four-bits way from him. Going to buy my wife some good ole lasses kisses with it. Gimme fifty cents worth of dem candy kisses."

"Fifty cents buys a mighty lot of candy kisses, Joe. Why don't you split it up and take some chocolate bars, too. They eat good, too."

"Yessuh, they do, but I wants all dat in kisses. I got a li'l boy chile home now. Tain't a week old yet, but he can suck a sugar tit and maybe eat one them kisses hisself."

Joe got his candy and left the store. The clerk turned to the next customer. "Wish I could be like these darkeys. Laughin' all the time. Nothin' worries 'em."

Back in Eatonville, Joe reached his own front door. There was the ring of singing metal on wood. Fifteen times. Missie May couldn't run to the door, but she crept there as quickly as she could.

"Joe Banks, I hear you chunkin' money in my doorway

You wait till I got my strength back, and I'm gonna fix you for dat."

The Taming of a Modern Shrew

by
RUTH D. TODD

THAT EDWARD REYNOLDS was the most daring young fellow in Liston was quite a settled fact. There was no mischief, no diabolical trick that could frighten him off. As a boy he was the terror of the town, for Liston was only a small town in southern Arkansas, where the major number of the inhabitants were Negroes.

Once, when he was quite a small lad, his companions had dared him to jump from the high town bridge into the stream below, and he had dared to do so with very fatal results.

That his neck hadn't been broken years before he arrived at manhood was no fault of his; however, he had come out of it all unscathed; a tall, perfectly built young man, as handsome as a god. His complexion was a reddish brown, his hair coarse, black, and as straight as an Indian's, and his eyes, which were the most striking feature about him, were large, fearless eyes, as black as night and sparkling with mischief, but a greater amount of daring.

Still, he was even-tempered, although his voice had a firm and commanding ring. He was certainly the most popular young fellow about town, and any one of the girls would have been proud to call him her "young man." But this youth, although not vain or egotistical, would have none of them, that is, excepting a certain beautiful damsel named Jennie Leigh, who, it seemed, would have none of him.

Jennie was the acknowledged belle of Liston. Her complexion was a trifle darker than Edward's, but she had soft, curly black hair, as fine and as glossy as silk, and large bewitching black eyes; in fact, many of the young men had been wont to declare that "Jennie Leigh's eyes always made a fellow feel deuced uncomfortable." She was fashionable, clever, witty, very charming, and possessed a temper that was, unlike Ed's, very uneven. In fact, when once aroused, she was a veritable shrew, though when things pleased her, there was not a young lady in Liston whose temper was so sweet or whose manner was gentler.

Edward was exceedingly fond of Jennie, in fact, had loved her when they were tots; and as a schoolgirl, he had carried no other girl's books but Jennie's to and from the village school; and after both had graduated from the high school, the intimacy had never decreased. So it was quite evident that they would someday marry, despite the fact that they were forever "scrapping" with each other.

It was quite amusing to see them together, for Ed's temper was so even, and his vein of humor so tantalizing, that he always managed to arouse Jennie's ire. He had often asked her to marry him, a thing which any other young man would not dare to even think of, and Jennie had flatly refused Ed s every proposal.

But this fearless young man's courage never deserted him; his will was indomitable, and he inwardly avowed that Jennie Leigh should wed none save him. That he would win her or devote his whole life to the attempt, he was determined. One day when they were attending a certain afternoon garden party, Jennie had looked so lovely in a beautiful gown of some pale blue, soft material that Ed had blurted out in his abrupt fashion: "Oh, Jennie, won't you be mine?"

"Ed Reynolds, you are the silliest person I know; Every blessed time you see me, you ask me to 'marry you, or be yours,' or something equally as stupid! You must think that I am going about looking for a husband, don't you?" she exclaimed impatiently.

"No, I did not think that, or I would have asked you nothing, because I'd have taken it for granted that I was your future spouse and led you to the minister's years ago,' answered Ed, gazing admiringly at her beautiful face and exquisite gown.

"Oh, you are just horrid, and sometimes I think I hate you," cried Jennie, angrily.

But Ed was so used to these angry outbursts of Jennie s that it would have seemed very unnatural if she had acted otherwise. They were seated on a little rustic seat quite out of "earshot," and Ed answered her, paying no attention whatever to her angry words:

"Gee, but that's a lovely dress you have on, Jennie. You look awfully sweet in it, Jen. I wish you belonged to me. Won't you tell me you will wed me, dear? Oh, please say yes, Jennie!" and he caught one of her soft little hands in his.

"Oh, Ed, don't be stupid; people are looking at us!" she cried, trying in vain to draw her hand away.

"Who cares?" answered he. "You know as well as they that I love you, Jen, have loved you all my life, and there isn't another girl that I'd even waste a thought on. I'm quite serious now, and if you send me away from you again, I'll do something desperate, I swear I will!"

"What will you do—commit suicide?" she asked, glancing mischievously up at him, for he had arisen now and with a slight frown upon his handsome face, and both hands thrust into his trousers pockets, he stood looking down upon her.

"Certainly not! Do you think I'm some darned idiot!" he exclaimed, indignantly.

"Men who are violently in love always commit suicide when the lady of their choice persistently refuses them."

"Let them, they're quite welcome, I'm sure. If they haven't got sense enough to bear up, they ought to die! What I'm going to do is to live and marry you."

"Oh, you are, are you? I'd like to see you without my consent."

"Oh, you'll consent all right."

"You are a conceited prig!" she cried, scornfully. "I'll show you whether I'll consent or not by accepting James Wilson the next time he asks me to marry him:?"

"What, that puppet! Has he asked you to marry him?"

"Why, of course he has. You are not the only person worthy of existence as yet," she exclaimed, indignantly.

"Why, confound him, if he even dares look at you again, I'll punch his head!" cried Ed, vehemently.

"Why, Ed Reynolds, you wouldn't dare. I'd hate you forever if you did such an ungentlemanly thing."

"I'd dare do anything for you. Oh, Jennie, dear Jennie, please say that you will be my own, my very own."

"You are absolutely incorrigible, Ed; do give me some rest."

"I will, when you promise to marry me, dear. Please say yes. Honest, I—I worship you. I don't know how on earth I can give you up. But I swear I'll leave town and never visit these parts again if you do not promise to marry me. I'm dead earnest this time. I know I've sworn to do all sorts of things time and again, but I'll—oh, Jennie, how can you be so cruel?"

"Cruel! Why I think I am extremely kind to you. There is not another person that I would allow to talk to me as you do, Ed Reynolds, but now I'll tell you what I will do."

"What will you do?"

"I'll marry you on one condition."

"Oh, name it! name it!" cried Ed, gladly.

"If you will write a novel or compose some poems worthy of notice, and have them published, I'll marry you— let's see—Easter."

"That's worse than cruel, Jennie. You know quite well that I'm not a literary chap, that I know nothing whatever of literature, and, er— you can't care anything for me if you ask me to do what you know is an impossibility."

"I never said I did care for you, did l?"

"But you do, don't you, Jen?"

"Do as I ask you to, and you will hear something that you have waited long to hear."

"Confound it, I'll try it, if I win or lose; I'd do anything to win you, dear Jennie."

And so it was announced that Jennie and Ed were to be married at Easter.

That was in September, and the last of March was drawing near before Ed was sure of winning his prize.

He knew that he would be very unsuccessful if he attempted such a serious thing as a novel, so he had tried his hand at poetry, but I'm afraid with very sad results. The following are specimens of his works:

It was a nice bright day in May,
The birds were warbling out their lay,
When everybody on that day
Would stare at my girl named May.

This terminated quite abruptly, as though the writer was disgusted with such rubbish. Then another:

Pathos
"My darling, I love you," the young man cried,
As he whispered these words to the maid at his side,
"If you will only say that you love me true,
I'll worship, adore you, my only dear Sue."

In fact this daring young man wasted a small fortune in stationery, with the most disgusting results, when it suddenly occurred to him to try his hand at nonsense poems, or stories in modern slang. So he wrote this:

To Jennie
There was once a young chap called Bennie,
Who loved a sweet maiden named Jennie,
Implored the lad, "Don't refuse me."
Cried the maid, "You confuse me,
For I don't know my mind, if I've any."

Said she, "I can't quite discover,
Why you are such a persistent young lover,
If you love me, dear Ben,
Win fame with the pen,
And I'll wed you instead of another."

"No, no!" cried the lad with a shiver,
That shook him and stirred up his liver,
"A pen I detest,
Ask me anything else,
For I'd rather jump into the river."

Then the maid opened her eyes wide in surprise,
"For a lover," said she, "you're unwise,
If you refuse my plan
You're a nutty young man,
And for a dunce you'd take the first prize."

The lad thought the maiden was joking,
But instead with anger she was choking,
"To the river," she said,
"For you've such a thick head,
That I'm sure it needs a good soaking."

Then the lad left the maiden quite sadly,
Said he, "I want you so badly,
That I'll try at the pen,
If I'm successful, why then,
Will you have me?" cried the maiden, "Oh, gladly!"

This lad's brain was as thick as fog,
It was even as thick as a log,

For he thought that dear Jen,
When she mentioned the pen,
Could mean nothing excepting the hog.

So this bug-housed young man named Ben
Built him an enormous big pen,
And then he spent
Every blessed red cent
Invested in hogs, he told Jen.

Then Jennie thought sure he was broke,
And she thought this a freak of a joke.
"He's quite crazy," she said,
"He's off of his head,"
And she laughed till she thought she would choke.

But Ben made a big pile of money,
And Jen said, "It's just too funny,
But wed you I must,
Or with laughter I'll bust."
And she kissed him, and called him her honey.

Then Ed wrote a story in modern slang, as follows:

To Jennie
Once upon a time there was a girl whose first name was Jennie. She was the swellest girl among the whole bunch with which she traveled. And there wasn't a chap in the whole neighborhood who wasn't dead gone on her. She wore such towering pompadours and such swell dresses she called gowns, and looked so much like a gorgeous queen, that all the other girls turned green with envy and the annoying disease called jealousy. And you can bet your life that this dusky damsel of the dreamy eyes was the only pebble on the beach. And as far as hot air was concerned, she could give more of that in ten minutes than any other girl could in fourteen hundred and ninety-eight hours. And she was quicker than lightning at spitting fire when a guy rubbed her the wrong way. She had no favorite guy that she doted on unless it was a swell-looking guy who lived near her, and who so persistently dogged this baby's cute little footsteps that she was forced to chew the taffy he gave her. This guy wore big-legged trousers and thought he looked wise and smart in rimless eye-glasses, which he donned after the maiden bade him do some intellectual stunts ere she would wed him.

It was a settled fact that this guy would win, so the other chaps all gave him a wide berth, but he failed to do these intellectual stunts and was about to give the whole business up as a bad job, when it rushed through his noggin that all girls liked loads of presents and a plenty of dough, and when these were rushed in upon her, she told him it was up to him to get the license, and she'd make the angel food with which to cholerize all of the guests, and the thing was completed in a swell church around the corner. Moral—Dough and a plenty of it is always the winning card.

He had no trouble to get Edson, the one and only colored editor in Liston, to promise to publish a nonsense poem or story in modern slang each week in his paper, and Ed hastened to the residence of his lady-love to tell her of his success.

"Oh, Ed, I think they are horrid!" cried Jennie, after she had read both poem and story.

"They are horrid, all right, but that's the only sort of literature now-a-days that makes a hit," answered Ed.

"I hope you are not going to have them published?" she asked anxiously.

"Of course I am. Do you suppose I'd give it up after seven long—almost intolerably long—months?"

"But surely you don't call this poetry or anything decent to read, even?"

"Sure—sure it is! It will make a hit all right."

"But why did you dedicate such horrid stuff to me? Oh, I think you are awful—just awful, and I hate you, Ed Reynolds!"

"You'll have to marry me, though," replied Ed, smiling triumphantly.

"I wouldn't marry you if there wasn't another man left, cried she, vehemently.

"You'll have to now. There's your promise that you'd wed me if I became successful, and I've leased a nonsense column in Edson's paper every week as long as I like to deal in literature," said Ed, quite complacently.

"Literature nothing. Why you know you wouldn't dare have such rubbish published, not if you cared anything for me."

"That's just why I'm going to have it published, because I think so much of you, I want the whole world to know. I shall sign my own name, Edward Benjamin Reynolds, in capital letters instead of a non-de-plume."

"Oh, you can't be serious, Ed."

"Never was more serious before in my life."

"Oh, Ed, please don't have it published, for my sake! The girls will all make the greatest joke of me. Oh, Ed, please don't!" she pleaded.

But Edward knew that he held the winning card in his hand, and he thought that now was the best time to get Jennie's consent to wed him in two weeks' time, so he firmly avowed that he'd have them published—that, in fact, Edson already had a type-written copy of them in his possession.

Then Jennie—the untamable, high-spirited Jennie Leigh —became quite meek and gentle, telling Ed that she would wed him on the morrow or whenever he wished if he would only promise her that he would not publish that awful stuff.

"But I won't marry you if you hate me, Jen," said Ed.

"You know that I love you, Ed, have always loved you and could never live without you, dear, and if you loved me, you would tear that paper up and throw it in the grate."

"Do you really love me, Jennie? Oh, Jennie, if I thought you cared enough to marry me Easter, I'd be the happiest man in Liston."

"And you wouldn't have them published?" Certainly not, darling."

"Then I am yours!" she cried, and Ed drew her to him, etc. etc.

On Easter morning, beneath an arch of lilies and surrounded by huge exotic plants in "St. James' Mission," Edward B. Reynolds and Jennie Leigh were happily wedded.

Emmy

by
<u>JESSIE REDMOND FAUSET</u>

"THERE ARE FIVE RACES," said Emmy confidently. "The white or Caucasian, the yellow or Mongolian, the red or Indian, the brown or Malay, and the black or Negro."

"Correct," nodded Miss Wenzel mechanically. "Now to which of the five do you belong?" And then immediately Miss Wenzel reddened.

Emmy hesitated. Not because hers was the only dark face in the crowded schoolroom, but because she was visualizing the pictures with which the geography had illustrated its information. She was not white, she knew that— nor had she almond eyes like the Chinese, nor the feathers which the Indian wore in his hair and which, of course, were to Emmy a racial characteristic. She regarded the color of her slim brown hands with interest—she had never thought of it before. The Malay was a horrid, ugly-looking thing with a ring in his nose. But he was brown, so she was, she supposed, really a Malay.

And yet the Hottentot, chosen with careful nicety to represent the entire Negro race, had on the whole a better appearance.

"I belong," she began tentatively, "to the black or Negro race."

"Yes," said Miss Wenzel with a sigh of relief, for if Emmy had chosen to ally herself with any other race except, of course, the white, how could she, teacher though she was set her straight without embarrassment? The recess bell rang, and she dismissed them with a brief but thankful You may pass."

Emmy uttered a sigh of relief, too, as she entered the schoolyard. She had been terribly near failing.

I was so scared," she breathed to little towheaded Mary Holborn. "Did you see what a long time I was answering? Guess Eunice Lecks

25

thought for sure I'd fail and she'd get my place."

"Yes, I guess she did," agreed Mary. "I'm so glad you didn't fail—but, oh, Emmy, didn't you mind?"

Emmy looked up in astonishment from the orange she was peeling.

"Mind what? Here, you can have the biggest half I don't like oranges anyway—sort of remind me of niter Mind what, Mary?"

"Why, saying you were black and"—she hesitated, her little freckled face getting pinker and pinker—"a Negro and all that before the class." And then mistaking the look on Emmy's face, she hastened on. "Everybody in Plainville says all the time that you're too nice and smart to be a—er —I mean, to be colored. And your dresses are so pretty and your hair isn't all funny either." She seized one of Emmy s hands—an exquisite member, all bronze outside, and within a soft pinky white.

"Oh, Emmy, don't you think if you scrubbed real hard you could get some of the brown off"

"But I don't want to," protested Emmy. "I guess my hands are as nice as yours, Mary Holborn. We're just the same, only you're white and I'm brown. But I don't see any difference. Eunice Lecks's eyes are green and yours are blue, but you can both see."

"Oh, well," said Mary Holborn, "if you don't mind—"

If she didn't mind—but why should she mind?

"Why should I mind, Archie?" she asked that faithful squire as they walked home in the afternoon through the pleasant "main" street. Archie had brought her home from school ever since she could remember. He was two years older than she; tall, strong, and beautiful, and her final arbiter.

Archie stopped to watch a spider.

"See how he does it, Emmy! See him bring that thread over! Gee, if I could swing a bridge across the pond as easy as that! What d'you say? Why should you mind? Oh, I don't guess there's anything for us to mind about. It's white people, they're always minding—I don't know why. If any of the boys in your class say anything to you, you let me know. I licked Bill Jennings the other day for calling me a 'guinea.' Wish I were a good, sure-enough brown like you, and then everybody'd know just what I am."

Archie's dear olive skin and aquiline features made his Negro ancestry difficult of belief

"But," persisted Emmy, "what difference does it make?"

"Oh, I'll tell you some other time," he returned vaguely. "Can't

26

you ask questions though? Look, it's going to rain. That means uncle won't need me in the field this afternoon. See here, Emmy, bet I can let you run ahead while I count fifteen, and then beat you to your house. Want to try?"

They reached the house none too soon, for the soft spring drizzle soon turned into gusty torrents. Archie was happy— he loved Emmy's house with the long, high rooms and the books and the queer foreign pictures. And Emmy had so many sensible playthings. Of course, a great big fellow of thirteen doesn't care for locomotives and blocks in the ordinary way, but when one is trying to work out how a bridge must be built over a lopsided ravine, such things are by no means to be despised. When Mrs. Carrel, Emmy's mother, sent Celeste to tell the children to come to dinner, they raised such a protest that the kindly French woman finally set them a table in the sitting room and left them to their own devices.

"Don't you love little fresh green peas?" said Emmy ecstatically. "Oh, Archie, won't you tell me now what difference it makes whether you are white or colored?" She peered into the vegetable dish. "Do you suppose Celeste would give us some more peas? There's only about a spoonful left."

"I don't believe she would," said the boy, evading the important part of her question. "There were lots of them to start with, you know. Look, if you take up each pea separately on your fork—like that—they'll last longer. It's hard to do, too. Bet I can do it better than you."

And in the exciting contest that followed both children forgot all about the "problem."

Miss Wenzel sent for Emmy the next day. Gently but insistently, and altogether from a mistaken sense of duty, she tried to make the child see wherein her lot differed from that of her white schoolmates. She felt herself that she hadn't succeeded very well. Emmy, immaculate in a white frock, her bronze elfin face framed in its thick curling black hair, alert with interest, had listened very attentively. She had made no comments till toward the end.

"Then because I'm brown," she had said, "I'm not as good as you." Emmy was at all times severely logical.

"Well, I wouldn't say that," stammered Miss Wenzel miserably. "You're really very nice, you know, especially nice for a colored girl, but—well, you're different."

27

Emmy listened patiently. "I wish you'd tell me how, Miss Wenzel, ' she began. "Archie Ferrers is different, too, isn't he? And yet he's lots nicer than almost any of the boys in Plainville. And he's smart, you know. I guess he's pretty poor—I shouldn't like to be that—but my mother isn't poor, and she's handsome. I heard Celeste say so, and she has beautiful clothes. I think, Miss Wenzel, it must be rather nice to be different."

It was at this point that Miss Wenzel had desisted and, tucking a little tissue-wrapped oblong into Emmy's hands, had sent her home.

"I don't think I did any good," she told her sister wonderingly. "I couldn't make her see what being colored meant."

"I don't see why you didn't leave her alone," said Hannah Wenzel testily. "I don't guess she'll meet with much prejudice if she stays here in central Pennsylvania. And If she goes away, she'll meet plenty of people who'll make it their business to see that she understands what being colored means. Those things adjust themselves."

"Not always," retorted Miss Wenzel, "and anyway, that child ought to know. She's got to have some of the wind taken out of her sails, someday, anyhow. Look how her mother dresses her. I suppose she does make pretty good money—I've heard that translating pays well. Seems so funny for a colored woman to be able to speak and write a foreign language." She returned to her former complaint.

"Of course it doesn't cost much to live here, but Emmy s clothes! White frocks all last winter, and a long red coat— broadcloth it was, Hannah. And big bows on her hair—she has got pretty hair, I must say."

"Oh, well," said Miss Hannah, "I suppose Celeste makes her clothes. I guess colored people want to look nice just as much as anybody else. I heard Mr. Holborn say Mrs. Carrel used to live in France; I suppose that's where she got all her stylish ways."

"Yes, just think of that," resumed Miss Wenzel vigorously, "a colored woman with a French maid. Though if it weren't for her skin, you'd never tell by her actions what she was. It's the same way with that Archie Ferrers, too, looking for all the world like some foreigner. I must say I like colored people to look and act like what they are."

She spoke the more bitterly because of her keen sense of failure. What she had meant to do was to show Emmy kindly—oh, very kindly—her proper place, and then, using the object in the little tissue-wrapped parcel as a sort of text, to preach a sermon on humility without aspiration.

The tissue-wrapped oblong proved to Emmy's interested eyes to contain a motto of Robert Louis Stevenson, entitled: "A Task"—the phrases picked out in red and blue and gold, under glass and framed in passepartout. Everybody nowadays has one or more of such mottoes in his house but the idea was new then to Plainville. The child read it through carefully as she passed by the lilac-scented "front yards." She read well for her age, albeit a trifle uncomprehendingly.

"To be honest, to be kind, to earn a little and to spend a little less;"—"there," thought Emmy, "is a semi-colon— let's see—the semicolon shows that the thought"—and she went on through the definition Miss Wenzel had given her and returned happily to her motto:

"To make upon the whole a family happier for his presence"—thus far the lettering was in blue. "To renounce when that shall be necessary and not be embittered"—this phrase was in gold. Then the rest went on in red: "To keep a few friends, but these without capitulation; above all, on the same given condition to keep friends with himself— here is a task for all that a man has of fortitude and delicacy.

"It's all about some man," she thought with a child's literalness. "Wonder why Miss Wenzel gave it to me? That big word, cap-it-u-la-tion"—she divided it off into syllables, doubtfully—"must mean to spell with capitals I guess. I'll say it to Archie some time."

But she thought it very kind of Miss Wenzel. And after she had shown it to her mother, she hung it up in the bay window of her little white room, where the sun struck it every morning.

Afterward Emmy always connected the motto with the beginning of her own realization of what color might mean. It took her quite a while to find it out, but by the time she was ready to graduate from the high school, she had come to recognize that the occasional impasse which she met now and then might generally be traced to color. This knowledge, however, far from embittering her, simply gave to her life keener zest. Of course she never met with any of the grosser forms of prejudice, and her personality was the kind to win her at least the respect and sometimes the wondering admiration of her schoolmates. For unconsciously she made them see that she was perfectly satisfied with being colored. She could never understand why anyone should think she would want to be white.

One day a girl—Elise Carter—asked her to let her copy her French verbs in the test they were to have later in the day. Emmy, who was both by nature and by necessity independent, refused bluntly.

"Oh, don't be so mean, Emmy," Elise had wailed. She hesitated. "If you'll let me copy them—I'll—I tell you what I'll do, I'll see that you get invited to our club spread Friday afternoon."

"Well I guess you won't," Emmy had retorted. "I'll probably be asked anyway. Most everybody else has been invited already."

Elise jeered. "And did you think as a matter of course that we'd ask you? Well, you have got something to learn."

There was no mistaking the "you."

Emmy took the blow pretty calmly for all its unexpectedness. "You mean," she said slowly, the blood showing darkly under the thin brown of her skin, "because I'm colored?"

Elise hedged—she was a little frightened at such directness.

"Oh, well, Emmy, you know colored folks can't expect to have everything we have, or if they do they must pay extra

"I—I see," said Emmy, stammering a little, as she always did when she was angry. "I begin to see for the first time why you think it's so awful to be colored. It's because you think we are willing to be mean and sneaky and"—with a sudden drop to schoolgirl vernacular—"soup-y. Why, Elise Carter, I wouldn't be in your old club with girls like you for worlds." There was no mistaking her sincerity.

"That was the day," she confided to Archie a long time afterward, "that I learned the meaning of making friends without capitulation.' Do you remember Miss Wenzel's motto, Archie?"

He assured her he did. "And of course you know, Emmy you were an awful brick to answer that Carter girl like that Didn't you really want to go to the spread"

"Not one bit," she told him vigorously, "after I found out why I hadn't been asked. And look, Archie, isn't it funny, just as soon as she wanted something, she didn't care whether I was colored or not."

Archie nodded. "They're all that way," he told her briefly.

"And if I'd gone, she'd have believed that all colored people were sort of—well, you know, 'meachin'—just like me. It s so odd the igno-rant way in which they draw their conclusions. Why, I remember reading the most interesting article in a magazine—the *Atlantic Monthly* I think it was. A woman had written it, and at this point she was condemning universal suffrage. And all of a sudden, without any warning, she spoke of that 'fierce, silly, amiable creature, the une-ducated Negro,' and—think of it, Archie—of 'his baser and sillier female.' It made me so angry. I've never forgotten it."

Archie whistled. "That was pretty tough," he acknowledged. I suppose the truth is," he went on smiling at her earnestness, "she has a colored cook who drinks."

"That's just it," she returned emphatically. "She probably has. But, Archie, just think of all the colored people we've both seen here and over in Newtown, too; some of them just as poor and ignorant as they can be. But not one of them is fierce or base or silly enough for that to be considered his chief characteristic. I'll wager that woman never spoke to fifty colored people in her life. No, thank you, if that's what it means to belong to the 'superior race,' I'll come back, just as I am, to the fiftieth reincarnation."

Archie sighed. "Oh, well, life is very simple for you. You see, you've never been up against it like I've been. After all, you've had all you wanted practically—those girls even came around finally in the high school and asked you into their clubs and things. While I—" He colored sensitively.

"You see, this plagued—er—complexion of mine doesn't tell anybody what I am. At first—and all along, too, if I let them—fellows take me for a foreigner of some kind—Spanish or something, and they take me up hail-fellow well-met. And then, if I let them know—I hate to feel I'm taking them in, you know, and besides that I can't help being curious to know what's going to happen—"

"What does happen?" interrupted Emmy, all interest.

"Well, all sorts of things. You take that first summer just before I entered preparatory school. You remember I was working at that camp in Cottage City. All the waiters were fellows just like me, working to go to some college or other. At first I was just one of them—swam with them, played cards—oh, you know, regularly chummed with them. We, the cook was a colored man—sure enough, colored you know—and one day one of the boys called him a—of course I couldn't tell you, Emmy, but he swore at him and called him a Nigger. And when I took up for him, the fellow said—he was angry, Emmy, and he said it as the worst insult he could think of—'Anybody would think you had black blood in your veins, too.'

" 'Anybody would think right'," I told him.

"Well?" asked Emmy.

He shrugged his shoulders. "That was all there was to it. The fellows dropped me completely—left me to the company of the cook, who was all right enough as cooks go, I suppose, but he didn't want me any more than I wanted him. And finally the manager came and told me he was sorry, but he guessed I'd have to go." He smiled grimly as at some unpleasant reminiscence.

"What's the joke?" his listener wondered.

"He also told me that I was the blankest kind of a blank fool—oh, you couldn't dream how he swore, Emmy. He said why didn't I leave well enough alone.

"And don't you know that's the thought I've had ever since—why not leave well enough alone?—and not tell people what I am. I guess you're different from me," he broke off wistfully, noting her look of disapproval; "you're so complete and satisfied in yourself. Just being Emilie Carrel seems to be enough for you. But you just wait until color keeps you from the thing you want the most, and you'll see."

"You needn't be so tragic," she commented succinctly. Outside of that one time at Cottage City, it doesn't seem to have kept you back."

For Archie's progress had been miraculous. In the seven years in which he had been from home, one marvel after another had come his way. He had found lucrative work each summer, he had got through his preparatory school in three years, he had been graduated number six from one of the best technical schools in the country— and now he had a position. He was to work for one of the biggest engineering concerns in Philadelphia.

This last bit of good fortune had dropped out of a clear sky. A guest at one of the hotels one summer had taken an interest in the handsome, willing bellboy and inquired into his history. Archie had hesitated at first, but finally, his eye alert for the first sign of dislike or superiority, he told the man of his Negro blood.

"If he turns me down," he said to himself boyishly, "I'll never risk it again."

But Mr. Robert Fallon—young, wealthy, and quixotic had become more interested than ever

"So it's all a gamble with you, isn't it? By George! How exciting your life must be—now white and now black— standing between ambition and honor, what? Not that I don't think you re doing the right thing—it's nobody's confounded business anyway. Look here, when you get through look me up. I may be able to put you wise to something. Here's my card. And say, mum's the word, and when you've made your pile, you can wake some fine morning and find yourself famous simply by telling what you are All rot, this beastly prejudice, I say."

And when Archie had graduated, his new friend, true to his word, had gotten for him from his father a letter of introduction to Mr. Nicholas Fields in Philadelphia, and Archie was placed. Young

Robert Fallon had gone laughing on his aimless, merry way.

"Be sure you keep your mouth shut, Ferrers, was his only enjoyment.

Archie, who at first had experienced some qualms, had finally completely acquiesced. For the few moments' talk with Mr. Fields had intoxicated him. The vision of work, plenty of it, his own chosen kind—and the opportunity to do it as a man—not an exception, but as a plain ordinary man among other men—was too much for him.

"It was my big chance, Emmy," he told her one day. He was spending his brief vacation in Plainville, and the two, having talked themselves out on other things, had returned to their old absorbing topic. He went on a little pleadingly, for she had protested. "I couldn't resist it. You don't know what it means to me. I don't care about being white in itself any more than you do—but I do care about a white man's chances. Don't let's talk about it anymore though; here it's the first week in September and I have to go the fifteenth. I may not be back till Christmas. I should hate to think that you—you were changed toward me, Emmy.

"I'm not changed, Archie," she assured him gravely, "only somehow it makes me feel that you're different. I can't quite look up to you as I used. I don't like the idea of considering the end justified by the means."

She was silent, watching the falling leaves flutter like golden butterflies against her white dress. As she stood there in the old-fashioned garden, she seemed to the boy's adoring eyes like some beautiful but inflexible bronze goddess

"I couldn't expect you to look up to me, Emmy, as though I were on a pedestal," he began miserably, "but I do want you to respect me, because—oh, Emmy, don't you see? I love you very much and I hope you will—I want you to—oh, Emmy, couldn't you like me a little? I— I've never thought ever of anyone but you. I didn't mean to tell you all about this now—I meant to wait until I really was successful, and then come and lay it all at your beautiful feet You're so lovely, Emmy. But if you despise me—" he was very humble.

For once in her calm young life Emmy was completely surprised. But she had to get to the root of things. "You mean, she faltered, "you mean you want"—she couldn't say it.

"I mean I want you to marry me," he said, gaining courage from her confusion. "Oh, have I frightened you, Emmy, dearest—of course you couldn't like me well enough for that all in a heap—it's different with me. I've always loved you, Emmy. But if you'd only think about

33

it."

Oh," she breathed, "there's Celeste. Oh, Archie, I don't know, it's all so funny. And we're so young. I couldn't really tell anything about my feelings anyway—you know, I've never seen anybody but you." Then as his face clouded— Oh, well, I guess even if I had, I wouldn't like him any better. Yes, Celeste, we're coming in. Archie, mother says you re to have dinner with us every night you're here, if you can."

There was no more said about the secret that Archie was keeping from Mr. Fields. There were too many other things to talk about—reasons why he had always loved Emmy; reasons why she couldn't be sure just yet; reasons why, if she were sure, she couldn't say yes

Archie hung between high hope and despair, while Emmy, it must be confessed, enjoyed herself, albeit innocently enough, and grew distractingly pretty. On the last day as they sat in the sitting room, gaily recounting childish episodes, Archie suddenly asked her again. He was so grave and serious that she really became frightened.

Oh, Archie, I couldn't—I don't really want to. It's so lovely just being a girl. I think I do like you—of course I like you lots. But couldn't we just be friends and keep going on—so?"

"No," he told her harshly, his face set and miserable no, we can't. And, Emmy—I'm not coming back any more —I couldn't stand it." His voice broke, he was fighting to keep back the hot boyish tears. After all he was only twenty-one. "I'm sorry I troubled you," he said proudly.

She looked at him pitifully. "I don't want you to go away forever, Archie," she said tremulously. She made no effort to keep back the tears. "I've been so lonely this last year since I've been out of school—you can't think."

He was down on his knees, his arms around her. "Emmy, Emmy, look up—are you crying for me, dear? Do you want me to come back—you do—you mean it? Emmy, you must love me, you do—a little." He kissed her slim fingers.

"Are you going to marry me? Look at me, Emmy—you are! Oh, Emmy, do you know I'm—I'm going to kiss you.

The stage came lumbering up not long afterward and bore him away to the train—triumphant and absolutely happy.

"My heart," sang Emmy rapturously as she ran up the broad, old-fashioned stairs to her room—"my heart is like a singing bird."

34

The year that followed seemed to her perfection. Archie's letters alone would have made it that. Emmy was quite sure that there had never been any other letters like them. She used to read them aloud to her mother.

Not all of them, though, for some were too precious for any eye but her own. She used to pore over them alone in her room at night, planning to answer them with an abandon equal to his own, but always finally evolving the same shy, almost timid epistle, which never failed to awaken in her lover's breast a sense equally of amusement and reverence. Her shyness seemed to him the most exquisite thing in the world—so exquisite, indeed, that he almost wished it would never vanish, were it not that its very disappearance would be the measure of her trust in him. His own letters showed plainly his adoration.

Only once had a letter of his caused a fleeting pang of misapprehension. He had been speaking of the persistent good fortune which had been his in Philadelphia.

"You can't think how lucky I am anyway," the letter ran on. "The other day I was standing on the corner of Fourth and Chestnut Streets at noon—you ought to see Chestnut Street, at twelve o'clock, Emmy—and someone came up, looked at me and said: 'Well, if it isn't Archie Ferrers!' And guess who it was, Emmy? Do you remember the Higginses who used to live over in Newtown? I don't suppose you ever knew them, only they were so queer looking that you must recall them. They were all sorts of colors from black with 'good' hair to yellow with the red, kinky kind. And then there was Maudet clearly a Higgins, and yet not looking like any of them, you know; perfectly white, with blue eyes and fair hair. Well, this was Maude, and, say, maybe she didn't look good. I couldn't tell you what she had on, but it was all right, and I was glad to take her over to the Reading Terminal and put her on a train to New York.

"I guess you're wondering where my luck is in all this tale, but you wait. Just as we started up the stairs of the depot, whom should we run into but young Peter Fields, my boss's son and heir, you know. Really, I thought I'd faint, and then I remembered that Maude was whiter than he in looks, and that there was nothing to give me away. He wanted to talk to us, but I hurried her off to her train. You know, it's a queer thing, Emmy; some girls are just naturally born stylish. Now there are both you and Maude Higgins, brought up from little things in a tiny inland town, and both of you able to give any of these city girls all sorts of odds in the matter of dressing."

Emmy put the letter down, wondering what had made her grow so cold.

"I wonder," she mused. She turned and looked in the glass to be confronted by a charming vision, slender—and dusky.

"I am black," she thought, "but comely." She laughed to herself happily. "Archie loves you, girl," she said to the face in the glass and put the little fear behind her. It met her insistently now and then, however, until the next week brought a letter begging her to get her mother to bring her to Philadelphia for a week or so.

"I can't get off till Thanksgiving, dearest, and I'm so lonely and disappointed. You know, I had looked forward so to spending the fifteenth of September with you—do you remember that date, sweetheart? I wouldn't have you come now in all this heat—you can't imagine how hot Philadelphia is, Emmy—but it's beautiful here in October. You'll love it, Emmy. It's such a big city—miles and miles of long, narrow streets, rather ugly, too, but all so interesting. You'll like Chestnut and Market Streets, where the big shops are, and South Street, teeming with Jews and colored people, though there are more of these last on Lombard Street. You never dreamed of so many colored people, Emmy Carrel—or such kinds.

"And then there are the parks and the theaters, and music and restaurants. And Broad Street late at night, all silent with gold, electric lights beckoning you on for miles and miles. Do you think your mother will let me take you out by yourself, Emmy? You'd be willing, wouldn't you?"

If Emmy needed more reassurance than that, she received it when Archie, a month later, met her and her mother at Broad Street station in Philadelphia. The boy was radiant. Mrs. Carrel, too, put aside her usual reticence, and the three were in fine spirits by the time they reached the rooms which Archie had procured for them on Christian Street. Once ensconced, the older woman announced her intention of taking advantage of the stores.

"I shall be shopping practically all day," she informed them. "I'll be so tired in the afternoons and evenings, Archie, that I'll have to get you to take my daughter off my hands."

Her daughter was delighted, but not more transparently so than her appointed cavalier. He was overjoyed at the thought of playing host and of showing Emmy the delights of city life.

"By the time I've finished showing you one-fifth of what I've planned, you'll give up the idea of waiting 'way till next October and marry me Christmas. Say, do it anyway, Emmy, won't you?" He waited tensely, but she only shook her head.

"Oh, I couldn't, Archie, and anyway you must show me first your wonderful city."

They did manage to cover a great deal of ground, though their mutual absorption made its impression on them very doubtful. Some things, though, Emmy never forgot. There was a drive one wonderful, golden October afternoon along the Wissahickon. Emmy, in her perfectly correct gray suit and smart little gray hat, held the reins—in itself a sort of measure of Archie's devotion to her, for he was wild about horses. He sat beside her ecstatic, ringing all the changes from a boy s nonsense to the most mature kind of seriousness. And always he looked at her with his passionate though reverent eyes. They were very happy.

There was some wonderful music, too, at the Academy. That was by accident though. For they had started for the theater—had reached there in fact. The usher was taking the tickets.

"This way, Emmy," said Archie. The usher looked up aimlessly, then, as his eyes traveled from the seeming young foreigner to the colored girl beside him, he flushed a little.

"Is the young lady with you?" he whispered politely enough. But Emmy, engrossed in a dazzling vision in a pink décolleté gown, would not in any event have heard him

"She is," responded Archie alertly. "What's the trouble, isn't tonight the seventeenth?"

The usher passed over this question with another—who had bought the tickets? Archie of course had, and told him so, frankly puzzled.

"I see. Well, I'm sorry," the man said evenly, "but these seats are already occupied, and the rest of the floor is sold out besides. There's a mistake somewhere. Now if you'll take these tickets back to the office, I can promise you they'll give you the best seats left in the balcony."

"What's the matter?" asked Emmy, tearing her glance from the pink vision at last. "Oh, Archie, you're hurting my arm; don't hold it that tight. Why—why are we going away from the theater? Oh, Archie, are you sick? You're just as white!"

"There was some mistake about the tickets," he got out, trying to keep his voice steady. "And a fellow in the crowd gave me an awful dig just then; guess that's why I'm pale. I'm so sorry, Emmy—I was so stupid, it's all my fault.

"What was the matter with the tickets?" she asked. "That's the

Bellevue-Stratford over there, isn't it? Then the Academy of Music must be near here. See how fast I'm learning? Let's go there; I've never heard a symphony concert. And, Archie, I've always heard that the best way to hear big music like that is at a distance, so get gallery tickets."

He obeyed her, fearful that if there were any trouble this time, she might hear it. Emmy enjoyed it all thoroughly, wondering a little, however, at his silence. "I guess he's tired," she thought. She would have been amazed to know his thoughts as he sat there staring moodily at the orchestra. "This damnation color business," he kept saying over and over.

That night as they stood in the vestibule of the Christian Street house, Emmy, for the first time, volunteered him a kiss. "Such a nice, tired boy," she said gently. Afterward he stood for a long time bareheaded on the steps looking at the closed door. Nothing he felt could crush him as much as that kiss had lifted him up.

Not even for lovers can a week last forever. Archie had kept till the last day what he considered his choicest bit of exploring. This was to take Emmy down into old Philadelphia and show her how the city had grown up from the waterfront—and by means of what tortuous self-governing streets. It was a sight at once dear and yet painful to his methodical, mathematical mind. They had explored Dock and Beach Streets and had got over into Shackamaxon, where he showed her Penn Treaty Park, and they had sat in the little pavilion overlooking the Delaware

Not many colored people came through this vicinity, and the striking pair caught many a wondering, as well as admiring, glance. They caught, too, the aimless, wandering eye of Mr. Nicholas Fields as he lounged, comfortably smoking, on the rear of a "Gunner's Run" car, on his way to Shackamaxon Ferry. Something in the young fellow's walk seemed vaguely familiar to him, and he leaned way out toward the sidewalk to see who that he knew could be over in this cheerless, forsaken locality.

"Gad!" he said to himself in surprise, "if it isn't young Ferrers, with a lady, too! Hello, why it's a colored woman! Ain't he a rip? Always thought he seemed too proper. Got her dressed to death, too; so that's how his money goes!" He dismissed the matter with a smile and a shrug of his shoulders.

Perhaps he would never have thought of it again had not Archie, rushing into the office a trifle late the next morning, caromed directly into him.

"Oh, it's you," he said, receiving his clerk's smiling apology. "What d'you mean by knocking into anybody like that? Mr. Fields was facetious with his favorite employees "Evidently your Shackamaxon trip upset you a little Where'd you get your black Venus, my boy? I'll bet you don't have one cent to rub against another at the end of a month. Oh, you needn't get red; boys will be boys, and everyone to his taste. Clarkson," he broke off, crossing to his secretary, "if Mr. Hunter calls me up, hold the 'phone and send over to the bank for me."

He had gone, and Archie, white now and shaken, entered his own little room. He sat down at the desk and sank his head in his hands. It had taken a moment for the insult to Emmy to sink in, but even when it did, the thought of his own false position had hold him back. The shame of it bit into him.

"I'm a coward," he said to himself, staring miserably at the familiar wall. "I'm a wretched cad to let him think that of Emmy—Emmy! and she the whitest angel that ever lived, purity incarnate." His cowardice made him sick. "I'll go and tell him," he said, and started for the door.

"If you do," whispered common sense, "you'll lose your job and then what would become of you? After all Emmy need never know."

"But I'll always know I didn't defend her," he answered back silently.

"He's gone out to the bank anyhow," went on the inward opposition. "What's the use of rushing in there and telling him before the whole board of directors?"

"Well, then, when he comes back," he capitulated, but he felt himself weaken.

But Mr. Fields didn't come back. When Mr. Hunter called him up, Clarkson connected him with the bank, with the result that Mr. Fields left for Reading in the course of an hour. He didn't come back for a week.

Meanwhile Archie tasted the depths of self-abasement. "But what am I to do?" he groaned to himself at nights. "If I tell him I'm colored, he'll kick me out, and if I go anywhere else, I'd run the same risk. If I'd only knocked him down! After all she'll never know, and I'll make it up to her. I'll be so good to her—dear little Emmy! But how could I know that he would take that view of it—beastly low mind he must have!" He colored up like a girl at the thought of it.

He passed the week thus, alternately reviling and defending himself. He knew now though that he would never have the courage to tell. The economy of the thing he decided was at least as important as the principle. And always he wrote to Emmy letters of such passionate adoration that the girl for all her natural steadiness was carried off her feet.

"How he loves me," she thought happily. "If mother is willing I believe—yes, I will—I'll marry him Christmas. But I won't tell him till he comes Thanksgiving."

When Mr. Fields came back he sent immediately for his son Peter. The two held some rather stormy consultations, which were renewed for several days. Peter roomed in town, while his father lived out at Chestnut Hill. Eventually Archie was sent for.

"You're not looking very fit, my boy," Mr. Fields greeted him; "working too hard, I suppose, over those specifications. Well, here's a tonic for you. This last week has shown me that I need someone younger than myself to take a hand in the business. I'm getting too old or too tired or something. Anyhow I'm played out.

"I've tried to make this young man here,"—with an angry glance at his son—"see that the mantle ought to fall on him, but he won't hear of it. Says the business can stop for all he cares; he's got enough money anyway. Gad, in my day young men liked to work, instead of dabbling around in this filthy social settlement business—with a lot of old maids."

Peter smiled contentedly. "Sally in our alley, what?" he put in diabolically. The older man glared at him, exasperated.

"Now look here, Ferrers," he went on abruptly. "I've had my eye on you ever since you first came. I don't know a thing about you outside of Mr. Fallon's recommendation, but I can see you've got good stuff in you—and what's more, you're a born engineer. If you had some money, I'd take you into partnership at once, but I believe you told me that all you had was your salary." Archie nodded.

"Well, now, I tell you what I'm going to do. I'm going to take you in as a sort of silent partner, teach you the business end of the concern, and in the course of a few years, place the greater part of the management in your hands You can see you won't lose by it. Of course I'll still be head and after I step out, Peter will take my place, though only nominally, I suppose."

He sighed; his son's business defection was a bitter point with him. But that imperturbable young man only nodded.

The boss guessed right the very first time," he paraphrased cheerfully. "You bet I'll be head in name only. Young Ferrers, there's just the man for the job. What d'you say, Archie?"

The latter tried to collect himself. "Of course I accept it, Mr. Fields, and I—I don't think you'll ever regret it." He actually stammered. Was there ever such wonderful luck?

"Oh, that's all right," Mr. Fields went on, "you wouldn't be getting this chance if you didn't deserve it. See here, what about your boarding out at Chestnut Hill for a year or two? Then I can lay my hands on you anytime, and you can get hold of things that much sooner. You live on Green Street, don't you? Well, give your landlady a month's notice and quit the first of December. A young man coming on like you ought to be thinking of a home anyway. Can't find some nice girl to marry you, what?"

Archie, flushing a little, acknowledged his engagement.

"Good, that's fine!" Then with sudden recollection— "Oh, so you're reformed. Well, I thought you'd get over that. Can't settle down too soon. A lot of nice little cottages out there at Chestnut Hill. Peter, your mother says she wishes you'd come out to dinner tonight. The youngest Wilton girl is to be there, I believe. Guess that's all for this afternoon, Ferrers."

Archie walked up Chestnut Street on air. "It's better to be born lucky than rich," he reflected. "But I'll be rich, too— and what a lot I can do for Emmy. Glad I didn't tell Mr. Fields now. Wonder what those 'little cottages' out to Chestnut Hill sell for. Emmy—" He stopped short, struck by a sudden realization.

"Why, I must be stark, staring crazy," he said to himself, standing still right in the middle of Chestnut Street. A stout gentleman whom his sudden stopping had seriously incommoded gave him, as he passed by, a vicious prod with his elbow. It started him on again. "If I hadn't clean forgotten all about it. Oh, Lord, what am I to do? Of course Emmy can't go out to Chestnut Hill to live—well, that would be a give-away. And he advised me to live out there for a year or two—and he knows I'm engaged, and—now—making more than enough to marry on."

He turned aimlessly down 19th Street and spying Rittenhouse Square, sat down in it. The cutting November wind swirled brown, crackling leaves right into his face, but he never saw one of them.

When he arose again, long after his dinner hour, he had made his decision. After all Emmy was a sensible girl; she knew he had only his salary to depend on. And, of course, he wouldn't have to stay out in Chestnut Hill forever. They could buy, or perhaps—he smiled proudly—even build now, far out in West Philadelphia, as far as possible away from Mr. Fields. He'd just ask her to postpone their marriage— perhaps for two years. He sighed a little, for he was very much in love.

"It seems funny that prosperity should make a fellow put off his happiness," he thought ruefully, swinging himself aboard a North 19th Street car.

He decided to go to Plainville and tell her about it—he could go up Saturday afternoon. "Let's see, I can get an express to Harrisburg, and a sleeper to Plainville, and come back Sunday afternoon. Emmy'll like a surprise like that." He thought of their improvised trip to the Academy and how she had made him buy gallery seats. "Lucky she has that little saving streak in her. She'll see through the whole thing like a brick." His simile made him smile. As soon as he reached home he scribbled her a note:

I m coming Sunday," he said briefly, "and I have something awfully important to ask you. I'll be there only from three to seven. 'When Time let's slip one little perfect hour,' that's that Omar thing you're always quoting, isn't it? Well, there'll be four perfect hours this trip."

All the way on the slow poky local from Harrisburg he pictured her surprise. "I guess she won't mind the postponement one bit," he thought with a brief pang. "She never was keen on marrying. Girls certainly are funny. Here she admits she's in love and willing to marry, and yet she s always hung fire about the date." He dozed fitfully.

As a matter of fact Emmy had fixed the date. "Of course," she said to herself happily, "the 'something important' is that he wants me to marry him right away. Well, I'll tell him that I will, Christmas. Dear old Archie coming all this distance to ask me that. I'll let him beg me two or three times first, and then I'll tell him. Won't he be pleased? I shouldn't be a bit surprised if he went down on his knees again." She flushed a little, thinking of that first wonderful time.

"Being in love is just—dandy," she decided. "I guess I'll wear my red dress."

Afterward the sight of that red dress always caused Emmy a pang of actual physical anguish. She never saw it without seeing, too, every detail of that disastrous Sunday afternoon. Archie had come— she had gone to the door to meet him— they had lingered happily in the hall a few moments, and then she had brought him in to her mother and Céleste.

The old French woman had kissed him on both cheeks. "See, then it's thou, my cherished one!" she cried ecstatically. "How long a time it is since thou art here."

Mrs. Carrel's greeting, though not so demonstrative, was no less sincere, and when the two were left to themselves "the cherished one" was radiant.

"My, but your mother can make a fellow feel welcome, Emmy. She doesn't say much, but what she does, goes."

Emmy smiled a little absently. The gray mist outside in the somber garden, the fire crackling on the hearth and casting ruddy shadows on Archie's hair, the very red of her dress, Archie himself— all this was making for her a picture, which she saw repeated on endless future Sunday afternoons in Philadelphia. She sighed contentedly.

"I've got something to tell you, sweetheart," said Archie.

"It's coming," she thought. "Oh, isn't it lovely! Of all the people in the world—he loves me, loves me!" She almost missed the beginning of his story. For he was telling her of Mr. Fields and his wonderful offer.

When she finally caught the drift of what he was saying, she was vaguely disappointed. He was talking business, in which she was really very little interested. The "saving streak" which Archie had attributed to her was merely sporadic and was due to a nice girl's delicacy at having money spent on her by a man. But, of course, she listened.

So you see the future is practically settled—there's only one immediate drawback," he said earnestly. She shut her eyes—it was coming after all.

He went on a little puzzled by her silence; "only one drawback, and that is that, of course, we can't be married for at least two years yet."

Her eyes flew open. "Not marry for two years! Why— why ever not?"

Even then he might have saved the situation by telling her first of his own cruel disappointment, for her loveliness as she sat there, all glowing red and bronze in the fire-lit dusk, smote him very strongly.

But he only floundered on.

"Why, Emmy, of course, you can see—you're so much darker than I—anybody can tell at a glance what you—er— are. He was crude, he

43

knew it, but he couldn't see how to help himself. 'And we'd have to live at Chestnut Hill, at first, right there near the Fields', and there'd be no way with you there to keep people from knowing that I— that— oh, confound it all—Emmy, you must understand! You don't mind, do you? You know you never were keen on marrying anyway. If we were both the same color—why Emmy, what is it?"

For she had risen and was looking at him as though he were someone entirely strange. Then she turned and gazed vacantly out the window. So that was it—the "something important—he was ashamed of her, of her color; he was always talking about a white man's chances. Why, of course, how foolish she'd been all along— how could he be white with her at his side? And she had thought he had come to urge her to marry him at once—the sting of it sent her head up higher. She turned and faced him, her beautiful silhouette distinctly outlined against the gray blur of the window. She wanted to hurt him—she was quite cool now.

"I have something to tell you, too, Archie," she said evenly. I've been meaning to tell you for some time. It seems I've been making a mistake all along. I don't really love you"—she was surprised dully that the words didn't choke her—"so, of course, I can't marry you. I was wondering how I could get out of it—you can't think how tiresome it's all been." She had to stop.

He was standing frozen, motionless like something carved.

"This seems as good an opportunity as any—oh, here s your ring," she finished, holding it out to him coldly. It was a beautiful diamond, small but flawless—the only thing he'd ever gone into debt for.

The statue came to life. "Emmy, you're crazy, he cried passionately, seizing her by the wrist. "You've got the wrong idea. You think I don't want you to marry me. What a cad you must take me for. I only asked you to postpone it a little while, so we'd be happier afterward. I'm doing it all for you, girl. I never dreamed—it's preposterous, Emmy And you can't say you don't love me—that's all nonsense!"

But she clung to her lie desperately.

"No, really, Archie, I don't love you one bit; of course I like you awfully—let go my wrist, you can think how strong you are. I should have told you long ago, but I hadn't the heart—and it really was interesting." No grand lady on the stage could have been more detached. He should know, too, how it felt not to be wanted.

He was at her feet now, clutching desperately, as she retreated, at her dress—the red dress she had donned so bravely. He couldn't

44

believe in her heartlessness. "You must love me, Emmy, and even if you don't, you must marry me anyway. Why, you promised—you don't know what it means to me, Emmy—it's my very life—I've never even dreamed of another woman but you! Take it back, Emmy, you can't mean it."

But she convinced him that she could. "I wish you'd stop, Archie," she said wearily; "this is awfully tiresome. And, anyway, I think you'd better go now if you want to catch your train."

He stumbled to his feet, the life all out of him. In the hall he turned around: "You'll say good-bye to your mother for me," he said mechanically. She nodded. He opened the front door. It seemed to close of its own accord behind him.

She came back into the sitting room, wondering why the place had suddenly grown so intolerably hot. She opened a window. From somewhere out of the gray mists came the strains of "Alice, Where Art Thou?" executed with exceeding mournfulness on an organ. The girl listened.

"That must be Willie Holborn," she thought; "no one else could play as wretchedly as that." She crossed heavily to the armchair and flung herself in it. Her mind seemed to go on acting as though it were clockwork and she were watching it.

Once she said: "Now this, I suppose, is what they call a tragedy." And again: "He did get down on his knees."

There was nothing detached or impersonal in Archie's consideration of his plight. All through the trip home, through the long days that followed and the still longer nights, he was in torment. Again and again he went over the scene

"She was making a plaything out of me," he chafed bitterly. "All these months she's been only fooling. And yet I wonder if she really meant it, if she didn't just do it to make it easier for me to be white. If that's the case, what an insufferable cad she must take me for. No, she couldn't have cared for me, because if she had, she'd have seen through it all right away."

By the end of ten days he had worked himself almost into a fever. His burning face and shaking hands made him resolve, as he dressed that morning, to 'phone the office that he was too ill to come to work.

"And I'll stay home and write her a letter that she'll have to answer." For although he had sent her one and sometimes two letters every day ever since his return, there had been no reply.

"She must answer that," he said to himself at length, when the late afternoon shadows were creeping in. He had torn up letter after letter—he had been proud and beseeching by turns. But in this last he had laid his very heart bare.

"And if she doesn't answer it"—it seemed to him he couldn't face the possibility. He was at the writing desk where her picture stood in its little silver frame. It had been there all that day. As a rule he kept it locked up, afraid of what it might reveal to his landlady's vigilant eye. He sat there, his head bowed over the picture, wondering dully how he should endure his misery.

Someone touched him on the shoulder.

"Gad, boy," said Mr. Nicholas Fields, "here I thought you were sick in bed, and come here to find you mooning over a picture. What's the matter? Won't the lady have you? Let's see who it is that's been breaking you up so."

Archie watched him in fascinated horror, while he picked up the photograph and walked over to the window. As he scanned it, his expression changed.

"Oh," he said, with a little puzzled frown and yet laughing, too, "it's your colored lady friend again. Won't she let you go? That's the way with these black women, once they get hold of a white man—bleed 'em to death. I don't see how you can stand them anyway; it's the Spanish in you, I suppose. Better get rid of her before you get married. Hello—" he broke off.

For Archie was standing menacingly over him. "If you say another word about that girl, I'll break every rotten bone in your body."

"Oh, come," said Mr. Fields, still pleasant, "isn't that going it a little too strong? Why, what can a woman like that mean to you?"

"She can mean," said the other slowly, "everything that the woman who has promised to be my wife ought to mean." The broken engagement meant nothing in a time like this.

Mr. Fields forgot his composure. "To be your wife! Why, you idiot, you—you'd ruin yourself—marry a Negro—have you lost your senses? Oh, I suppose it's some of your crazy foreign notions. In this country white gentlemen don't marry colored women."

Archie had not expected this loophole. He hesitated, then with a shrug he burnt all his bridges behind him. One by one he saw his ambitions flare up and vanish

"No, you're right," he rejoined. "White gentlemen don't but colored men do." Then he waited calmly for the avalanche.

It came. "You mean," said Mr. Nicholas Fields, at first with only wonder and then with growing suspicion in his voice, "you mean that you're colored?" Archie nodded and watched him turn into a maniac.

"Why, you low-life young blackguard, you—" he swore horribly. And you've let me think all this time—" He broke off again, hunting for something insulting enough to say. "You Nigger!" he hurled at him. He really felt there was nothing worse, so he repeated it again and again.

"I think," said Archie, "that that will do. I shouldn't like to forget myself, and I'm in a pretty reckless mood today. You must remember, Mr. Fields, you didn't ask me who I was, and I had no occasion to tell you. Of course I won't come back to the office."

"If you do," said Mr. Fields, white to the lips, "I'll have you locked up if I have to perjure my soul to find a charge against you. I'll show you what a white man can do— you—"

But Archie had taken him by the shoulder and pushed him outside the door.

"And that's all right," he said to himself with a sudden heady sense of liberty. He surveyed himself curiously in the mirror. "Wouldn't anybody think I had changed into some horrible ravening beast. Lord, how that one little word changed him." He ruminated over the injustice—the petty foolish injustice of the whole thing.

"I don't believe," he said slowly, "it's worthwhile having a white man's chances if one has to be like that. I see what Emmy used to be driving at now." The thought of her sobered him.

"If it should be on account of my chances that you're letting me go," he assured the picture gravely, "it's all quite unnecessary, for I'll never have another opportunity like that."

In which he was quite right. It even looked as though he couldn't get any work at all along his own line. There was no demand for colored engineers.

"If you keep your mouth shut," one man said, "and not let the other clerks know what you are, I might try you for awhile." There was nothing for him to do but accept. At the end of two weeks—the day before Thanksgiving—he found out that the men beside him, doing exactly the same kind of work as his own, were receiving for it five dollars more a week. The old injustice based on color had begun to hedge him in. It seemed to him that his unhappiness and humiliation were more than he could stand.

But at least his life was occupied. Emmy, on the other hand, saw her own life stretching out through endless vistas of empty, useless days. She grew thin and listless, all the brightness and vividness of living toned down for her into one gray, flat monotony. By Thanksgiving Day the strain showed its effects on her very plainly.

Her mother, who had listened in her usual silence when her daughter told her the cause of the broken engagement, tried to help her.

"Emmy," she said, "you're probably doing Archie an injustice. I don't believe he ever dreamed of being ashamed of you. I think it is your own pride that is at fault. You'd better consider carefully—if you are making a mistake, you'll regret it to the day of your death. The sorrow of it will never leave you."

Emmy was petulant. "Oh, mother, what can you know about it? Celeste says you married when you were young, even younger than I—married to the man you loved, and you were with him, I suppose, till he died. You couldn't know how I feel." She fell to staring absently out the window. It was a long time before her mother spoke again.

"No, Emmy," she finally began again very gravely, "I wasn't with your father till he died. That is why I'm speaking to you as I am. I had sent him away—we had quarrelled —oh, I was passionate enough when I was your age, Emmy. He was jealous—he was a West Indian—I suppose Celeste has told you—and one day he came past the sitting room— it was just like this one, overlooking the garden. Well, as he glanced in the window, he saw a man, a white man, put his arms around me and kiss me. When he came in through the side door, the man had gone. I was just about to explain— no, tell him— for I didn't know he had seen me when he began." She paused a little, but presently went on in her even, dispassionate voice:

"He was furious, Emmy; oh, he was so angry, and he accused me—oh, my dear! He was almost insane. But it was really because he loved me. And then I became angry and I wouldn't tell him anything. And finally, Emmy, he struck me—you mustn't blame him, child; remember, it was the same spirit showing in both of us, in different ways. I was doing all I could to provoke him by keeping silence, and he merely retaliated in his way. The blow wouldn't have harmed a little bird. But—well, Emmy, I think I must have gone crazy. I ordered him from the house—it had been my mother's—and I told him never, never to let me see him again." She smiled drearily.

"I never did see him again. After he left, Celeste and I packed up our things and came here to America. You were the littlest thing,

48

Emmy. You can't remember living in France at all, can you? Well, when your father found out where I was, he wrote and asked me to forgive him and to let him come back. 'I am on my knees,' the letter said. I wrote and told him yes—I loved him, Emmy; oh, child, you with your talk of color; you don't know what love is. If you really loved Archie, you'd let him marry you and lock you off, away from all the world, just so long as you were with him.

"I was so happy," she resumed. "I hadn't seen him for two years. Well, he started—he was in Haiti then; he got to New York safely and started here. There was a wreck—Just a little one—only five people killed, but he was one of them. He was so badly mangled, they wouldn't even let me see him."

"Oh!" breathed Emmy. "Oh, Mother!" After a long time she ventured a question. "Who was the other man, mother?"

"The other man? Oh! That was my father; my mother's guardian, protector, everything, but not her husband. She was a slave, you know, in New Orleans, and he helped her to get away. He took her to Haiti first, and then, afterward, sent her over to France, where I was born. He never ceased in his kindness. After my mother's death, I didn't see him for ten years, not till after I was married. That was the time Emile— you were named for your father, you know—saw him kiss me. Mr. Pechegru, my father, was genuinely attached to my mother, I think, and had come after all these years to make some reparation. It was through him I first began translating for the publishers. You know yourself how my work has grown."

She was quite ordinary and matter-of-fact again. Suddenly her manner changed.

"I lost him when I was twenty-two. Emmy—think of it— and my life has been nothing ever since. That's why I want you to think—to consider—" She was weeping passionately now

Her mother in tears! To Emmy it was as though the world lay in ruins about her feet.

As it happened, Mrs. Carrel's story only plunged her daughter into deeper gloom.

"It couldn't have happened at all if we hadn't been colored," she told herself moodily. "If grandmother hadn't been colored, she wouldn't have been a slave, and if she hadn't been a slave—That's what it is, color—color—it's wrecked mother's life, and now it's wrecking mine."

She couldn't get away from the thought of it. Archie's words, said so long ago, came back to her: "Just wait till color keeps you from the thing you want the most," he had told her.

"It must be wonderful to be white," she said to herself, staring absently at the Stevenson motto on the wall of her little room She went up close and surveyed it. "If only I weren't colored," she thought. She checked her self angrily, enveloped by a sudden sense of shame. "It doesn't seem as though I could be the same girl."

A thin ray of cold December sunlight picked out from the motto a little gilded phrase: "To renounce when that shall be necessary and not be embittered." She read it over and over and smiled whimsically.

"I've renounced—there's no question about that," she thought, "but no one could expect me not to be bitter."

If she could just get up strength enough, she reflected, as the days passed by, she would try to be cheerful in her mother's presence. But it was so easy to be melancholy.

About a week before Christmas her mother went to New York. She would see her publishers and do some shopping and would be back Christmas Eve. Emmy was really glad to see her go.

"I'll spend that time in getting myself together," she told herself, "and when mother comes back, I'll be all right." Nevertheless, for the first few days she was, if anything, more listless than ever. But Christmas Eve and the prospect of her mother's return gave her a sudden brace.

"Without bitterness," she kept saying to herself, "to renounce without bitterness." Well, she would—she would. When her mother came back, she should be astonished. She would even wear the red dress. But the sight of it made her weak; she couldn't put it on. But she did dress herself very carefully in white, remembering how gay she had been last Christmas Eve. She had put mistletoe in her hair, and Archie had taken it out.

"I don't have to have mistletoe," he had whispered to her proudly.

In the late afternoon she ran out to Holborn's. As she came back 'round the corner, she saw the stage drive away. Her mother, of course, had come. She ran into the sitting room wondering why the door was closed.

"I will be all right," she said to herself, her hand on the knob, and stepped into the room—to walk straight into Archie's arms.

She clung to him as though she could never let him go.

"Oh, Archie, you've come back, you really wanted me.

He strained her closer. "I've never stopped wanting you," he told her, his lips on her hair.

Presently, when they were sitting by the fire, she in the armchair and he at her feet, he began to explain. She would not listen at first, it was all her fault, she said.

"No, indeed," he protested generously, "it was mine. I was so crude; it's a wonder you can care at all about anyone as stupid as I am. And I think I was too ambitious—though in a way it was all for you, Emmy; you must always believe that. But I'm at the bottom rung now, sweetheart; you see, I told Mr. Fields everything and—he put me out."

"Oh, Archie," she praised him, "that was really noble, since you weren't obliged to tell him."

"Well, but in one sense I was obliged to—to keep my self-respect, you know. So there wasn't anything very noble about it after all." He couldn't tell her what had really happened. "I'm genuinely poor now, dearest, but your mother sent for me to come over to New York. She knows some pretty all-right people there—she's a wonderful woman, Emmy—and I'm to go out to the Philippines. Could you—do you think you could come out there, Emmy?"

She could, she assured him, go anywhere. "Only don't let it be too long, Archie—I—"

He was ecstatic. "Emmy—you—you don't mean you would be willing to start out there with me, do you? Why, that's only three months off. When—" He stopped, peering out the window. "Who is that coming up the path?"

"It's Willie Holborn," said Emmy. "I suppose Mary sent him around with my present. Wait, I'll let him in."

But it wasn't Willie Holborn, unless he had been suddenly converted into a small and very grubby special-delivery boy.

"Mr. A. Ferrers," he said laconically, thrusting a book out at her. "Sign here."

She took the letter back into the pleasant room, and A Ferrers, scanning the postmark, tore it open. "It's from my landlady; she's the only person in Philadelphia who knows where I am. Wonder what's up?" he said. "I know I didn't forget to pay her my bill. Hello, what's this?" For within was a yellow envelope—a telegram

Together they tore it open

"Don't be a blooming idiot," it read; "the governor says come back and receive apologies and accept job. Merry Christmas. Peter

51

Fields."

"Oh," said Emmy, "isn't it lovely? Why does he say 'receive apologies,' Archie?"

"Oh, I don't know," he quibbled, reflecting that if Peter hadn't said just that, his return would have been as impossible as ever. "It's just his queer way of talking. He's the funniest chap! Looks as though I wouldn't have to go to the Philippines after all. But that doesn't alter the main question How soon do you think you can marry me, Emmy?"

His voice was light, but his eyes—

"Well," said Emmy bravely, "what do you think of Christmas?"

52

The Two Offers

by
<u>FRANCES ELLEN WATKINS HARPER</u>

"WHAT IS THE MATTER with you, Laura, this morning? I have been watching you this hour, and in that time you have commenced a half-dozen letters and torn them all up. What matter of such grave moment is puzzling your dear little head, that you do not know how to decide?"

"Well, it is an important matter; I have two offers for marriage, and I do not know which to choose.

"I should accept neither, or to say the least, not at present."

"Why not?"

"Because I think a woman who is undecided between two offers has not love enough for either to make a choice; and in that very hesitation, indecision, she has a reason to pause and seriously reflect, lest her marriage, instead of being an affinity of souls or a union of hearts, should only be a mere matter of bargain and sale, or an affair of convenience and selfish interest."

"But I consider them both very good offers, just such as many a girl would gladly receive. But to tell you the truth, I do not think that I regard either as a woman should the man she chooses for her husband. But then if I refuse there is the risk of being an old maid, and that is not to be thought of."

"Well, suppose there is? Is that the most dreadful fate that can befall a woman? Is there not more intense wretchedness in an ill-assorted marriage, more utter loneliness in a loveless home, than in the lot of the old maid who accepts her earthly mission as a gift from God and strives to walk the path of life with earnest and unfaltering steps?"

Oh! what a little preacher you are. I really believe that you were cut out for an old maid—that when nature formed you, she put in a double portion of intellect to make up for a deficiency of love; and yet you are kind and affectionate. But I do not think that you know anything of the grand, overmastering passion, or the deep necessity of woman s heart for loving."

"Do you think so?" resumed the first speaker, and bending over her work she quietly applied herself to the knitting that had lain neglected by her side during this brief conversation. But as she did so, a shadow flitted over her pale and intellectual brow, a mist gathered in her eyes, and a slight quivering of the lips revealed a depth of feeling to which her companion was a stranger.

But before I proceed with my story, let me give you a slight history of the speakers. They were cousins who had met life under different auspices. Laura Lagrange was the only daughter of rich and indulgent parents who had spared no pains to make her an accomplished lady. Her cousin, Janette Alston, was the child of parents rich only in goodness and affection. Her father had been unfortunate in business and, dying before he could retrieve his fortunes, left his business in an embarrassed state. His widow was unacquainted with his business affairs, and when the estate was settled, hungry creditors had brought their claims, and the lawyers had received their fees, she found herself homeless and almost penniless, and she, who had been sheltered in the warm clasp of loving arms, found them too powerless to shield her from the pitiless pelting storms of adversity. Year after year she struggled with poverty and wrestled with want, till her toil-worn hands became too feeble to hold the shattered chords of existence, and her tear-dimmed eyes grew heavy with the slumber of death.

Her daughter had watched over her with untiring devotion, had closed her eyes in death and gone out into the busy, restless world, missing a precious tone from the voices of earth, a beloved step from the paths of life. Too self-reliant to depend on the charity of relations, she endeavored to support herself by her own exertions, and she had succeeded. Her path for a while was marked with struggle and trial, but instead of uselessly repining, she met them bravely, and her life became a thing not of ease and indulgence, but of conquest, victory, and accomplishments. At the time when this conversation took place, the deep trials of her life had passed away. The achievements of her genius had won her a position in the literary world, where she shone as one of its bright particular stars. And with her fame came a competence of worldly means, which gave her leisure for improvement

54

and the riper development of her rare talents. And she, that pale intellectual woman, whose genius gave life and vivacity to the social circle and whose presence threw a halo of beauty and grace around the charmed atmosphere in which she moved, had at one period of her life known the mystic and solemn strength of an all-absorbing love. Years faded into the misty past had seen the kindling of her eye, the quick flushing of her cheek, and the wild throbbing of her heart at tones of a voice long since hushed to the stillness of death. Deeply, wildly, passionately, she had loved . . . This love quickened her talents, inspired her genius, and threw over her life a tender and spiritual earnestness.

And then came a fearful shock, a mournful waking from that "dream of beauty and delight." A shadow fell around her path; it came between her and the object of her heart's worship. First a few cold words, estrangement, and then a painful separation: the old story of woman's pride . . . And thus faded out from that young heart her bright, brief and saddened dream of life. Faint and spirit-broken, she turned from the scenes associated with the memory of the loved and lost. She tried to break the chain of sad associations that bound her to the mournful past; and so . . . her genius gathered strength from suffering, and wondrous power and brilliancy from the agony she hid within the desolate chambers of her soul . . . and turning, with an earnest and shattered spirit, to life's duties and trials, she found a calmness and strength that she had only imagined m her dreams of poetry and song.

We will now pass over a period of ten years, and the cousins have met again. In that calm and lovely woman, in whose eyes is a depth of tenderness tempering the flashes of her genius, whose looks and tones are full of sympathy

and love, we recognize the once smitten and stricken Janette Alston. The bloom of her girlhood had given way to a higher type of spiritual beauty, as if some unseen hand had been polishing and refining the temple in which her lovely spirit found its habitation. . .

Never in the early flush of womanhood, when an absorbing love had lit up her eyes and glowed in her life, had she appeared so interesting as when, with a countenance which seemed overshadowed with a spiritual light, she bent over the deathbed of a young woman just lingering at the shadowy gates of the unseen land.

"Has he come?" faintly but eagerly exclaimed the dying woman. "Oh! how I have longed for his coming, and even in death he forgets me."

"Oh, do not say so, dear Laura. Some accident may have detained him, said Janette to her cousin; for on that bed from whence she will never rise, lies the once beautiful and lighthearted Laura Lagrange, the brightness of whose eyes had long since been dimmed with tears, and whose voice had become like a harp whose every chord is tuned to sadness— whose faintest thrill and loudest vibrations are but the variations of agony. A heavy hand was laid upon her once warm and bounding heart, and a voice came whispering through her soul that she must die. But to her the tidings was a message of deliverance—a voice hushing her wild sorrows to the calmness of resignation and hope.

Life had grown so weary upon her head—the future looked so hopeless—she had no wish to tread again the track where thorns had pierced her feet and clouds overcast her sky, and she hailed the coming of death's angel as the footsteps of a welcome friend. And yet, earth had one object so very dear to her weary heart. It was her absent and recreant husband; for, since that conversation [ten years earlier], she had accepted one of her offers and become a wife. But before she married she learned that great lesson of human experience and woman's life—to love the man who bowed at her shrine, a willing worshipper.

He had a pleasing address, raven hair, flashing eyes, a voice of thrilling sweetness, and lips of persuasive eloquence; and being well versed in the ways of the world, he won his way to her heart and she became his bride, and he was proud of his prize. Vain and superficial in his character, he looked upon marriage not as a divine sacrament for the soul's development and human progression, but as the title deed that gave him possession of the woman he thought he loved. But alas for her, the laxity of his principles had rendered him unworthy of the deep and undying devotion of a pure-hearted woman. But, for a while, he hid from her his true character, and she blindly loved him, and for a short period was happy in the consciousness of being beloved. Though sometimes a vague unrest would fill her soul, when, overflowing with a sense of the good, the beautiful, and the true, she would turn to him but find no response to the deep yearnings of her soul—no appreciation of life s highest realities, its solemn grandeur and significant importance. Their souls never met, and soon she found a void in her bosom that his earthborn love could not fill. He did not satisfy the wants of her mental and moral nature: between him and her there was no affinity of minds, no intercommunion of souls.

Talk as you will of woman's deep capacity for loving—of the strength of her affectionate nature. I do not deny it. But will the mere possession of any human love fully satisfy all the demands of her whole being? You may paint her in poetry or fiction as a frail vine, clinging to her brother man or support and dying when deprived of it, and all this may sound well enough to please the imaginations of schoolgirls, or lovelorn maidens. But woman—the true woman— if you would render her happy, it needs more than the mere development of her affectionate nature. Her conscience should be enlightened, her faith in the true and right established, and scope given to her heaven-endowed and God-given faculties. The true aim of female education should be, a development of not one or two but all the faculties of the human soul, because no perfect womanhood is developed by imperfect culture. Intense love is often akin to intense suffering, and to trust the whole wealth of woman's nature on the frail bark of human love may often be like trusting a cargo of gold and precious gems to a bark that has never battled with the storm or buffeted the waves. Is it any wonder, then, that so many life-barks . . . are stranded on the shoals of existence, mournful beacons and solemn warnings for the thoughtless, to whom marriage is a careless and hasty rushing together of the affections? Alas that an institution so fraught with good for humanity should be so perverted, and that state of life which should be filled with happiness become so replete with misery. And this was the fate of Laura Lagrange.

For a brief period after her marriage her life seemed like a bright and beautiful dream, full of hope and radiant with joy. And then there came a change: he found other attractions that lay beyond the pale of home influences. The gambling saloon had power to win him from her side, he had lived in an element of unhealthy and unhallowed excitements, and the society of a loving wife, the pleasures of a well-regulated home, were enjoyments too tame for one whose tastes were accustomed to the pleasures of sin. There were charmed houses of vice built upon dead men's loves where, amid a flow of song, laughter, wine, and careless mirth, he would spend hour after hour, forgetting the cheek that was paling through his neglect, heedless of the tear-dimmed eyes peering anxiously into the darkness , waiting or watching his return.

The influence of old associations was upon him. In early life, home had been to him a place of ceilings and walls, not a true home built upon goodness, love, and truth. It was a place where velvet carpets hushed his tread, where images of loveliness and beauty, invoked into being by painter s art and sculptor's skill, pleased the eye and gratified the taste, where magnificence surrounded his way and costly clothing adorned his person; but it was not the place for the true culture and right development of his soul. His father had been too much engrossed in making money and his mother in spending it, in striving to maintain a fashionable position in society and shining in the eyes of the world, to give the proper direction to the character of their wayward and impulsive son. His mother put beautiful robes upon his body but left ugly scars upon his soul; she pampered his appetite but starved his spirit . . .

That parental authority which should have been preserved as a string of precious pearls, unbroken and unscattered, was simply the administration of chance. At one time obedience was enforced by authority, at another time by flattery and promises, and just as often it was not enforced.

His early associations were formed as chance directed, and from his want of home training, his character received a bias, his life a shade, which ran through every avenue of his existence and darkened all his future hours . . .

Before a year of his married life had waned, his young wife had learned to wait and mourn his frequent and uncalled-for absence. More than once had she seen him come home from his midnight haunts, the bright intelligence of his eye displaced by the drunkard's stare, and his manly gait changed to the inebriate's stagger; and she was beginning to know the bitter agony that is compressed in the mournful words "drunkard's wife."

And then there came a bright but brief episode in her experience. The angel of life gave to her existence a deeper meaning and loftier significance: she sheltered in the warm clasp of her loving arms a dear babe, a precious child whose love filled every chamber of her heart. . . . How many lonely hours were beguiled by its winsome ways, its answering smiles and fond caresses! How exquisite and solemn was the feeling that thrilled her heart when she clasped the tiny hands together and taught her dear child to call God 'Our Father"!

What a blessing was that child! The father paused in his headlong career, awed by the strange beauty and precocious intellect of his child; and the mother's life had a better expression through her ministrations of love. And then there came hours of bitter anguish, shading the sunlight of her home and hushing the music of her heart. The angel of death bent over the couch of her child and beckoned it away. Closer and closer the mother strained her child to her wildly heaving breast and struggled with the heavy hand that lay upon its heart. Love and agony contended with death . . .

But death was stronger than love and mightier than agony and won the child for the land of crystal founts and deathless flowers, and the poor stricken mother sat down beneath the shadow of her mighty grief, feeling as if a great light had gone out from her soul and that the sunshine had suddenly faded around her path. She turned in her deep anguish to the father of her child, the loved and cherished dead. For a while his words were kind and tender, his heart seemed subdued, and his tenderness fell upon her worn and weary heart like rain on perishing flowers, or cooling waters to lips all parched with thirst and scorched with fever. But the change was evanescent; the influence of unhallowed associations and evil habits had vitiated and poisoned the springs of his existence. They had bound him in their meshes, and he lacked the moral strength to break his fetters and stand erect in all the strength and dignity of a true manhood, making life's highest excellence his ideal and striving to gain it.

And yet moments of deep contrition would sweep over him, when he would resolve to abandon the wine cup forever, when he was ready to forswear the handling of another card, and he would try to break away from the associations that he felt were working his ruin. But when the hour of temptation came, his strength was weakness, his earnest purposes were cobwebs, his well-meant resolutions ropes of sand—and thus passed year after year of the married life of Laura Lagrange. She tried to hide her agony from the public gaze, to smile when her heart was almost breaking. But year after year her voice grew fainter and sadder, her once light and bounding step grew slower and flattering.

Year after year she wrestled with agony and strove with despair, till the quick eyes of her brother read, in the paling of her cheek and the dimming eyes the secret anguish of her worn and weary spirit. On that wan, sad face he saw the death tokens, and he knew the dark wing of the mystic angel swept cold around her path.

"Laura," said her brother to her one day, "you are not well, and I think you need our mother's tender care and nursing. You are daily losing strength, and if you will go, I will accompany you."

At first she hesitated; she shrank almost instinctively from presenting that pale, sad face to the loved ones at home . . . But then a deep yearning for home sympathy woke within her a passionate longing for love's kind words, for tenderness and heart support, and she resolved to seek the home of her childhood and lay her weary head upon her mother's bosom, to be folded again in her loving arms, to lay that poor, bruised and aching heart where it might beat and throb closely to the loved ones at home.

A kind welcome awaited her. All that love and tenderness could devise was done to bring the bloom to her cheek and the light to her eye. But it was all in vain; hers was a disease that no medicine could cure, no earthly balm would heal. It was a slow wasting of the vital forces, the sickness of the soul. The unkindness and neglect of her husband lay like a leaden weight upon her heart . . .

And where was he that had won her love and then cast it aside as a useless thing, who rifled her heart of its wealth and spread bitter ashes upon its broken altars? He was lingering away from her when the death damps were gathering on her brow, when his name was trembling on her lips! Lingering away! when she was watching his coming, though the death films were gathering before her eyes and earthly things were fading from her vision.

"I think I hear him now," said the dying woman, "surely that is his step," but the sound died away in the distance.

Again she started from an uneasy slumber: "That is his voice! I am so glad he has come."

Tears gathered in the eyes of the sad watchers by that dying bed, for they knew that she was deceived. He had not returned. For her sake they wished his coming. Slowly the hours waned away, and then came the sad, soul-sickening thought that she was forgotten, forgotten in the last hour of human need, forgotten when the spirit, about to be dissolved, paused for the last time on the threshold of existence, a weary watcher at the gates of death.

"He has forgotten me," again she faintly murmured, and the last tears she would ever shed on earth sprang to her mournful eyes, and . . . a few broken sentences issued from her pale and quivering lips. They were prayers for strength, and earnest pleading for him who had desolated her young life by turning its sunshine to shadows, its smiles to tears.

"He has forgotten me," she murmured again, "but I can bear it; the bitterness of death is passed, and soon I hope to exchange the shadows of death for the brightness of eternity, the rugged paths of life for the golden streets of glory, and the care and turmoils of earth for the peace and rest of heaven."

Her voice grew fainter and fainter; they saw the shadows that never deceive flit over her pale and faded face and knew that the death angel waited to soothe their weary one to rest, to calm the throbbing of her bosom and cool the fever of her brain. And amid the silent hush of their grief, the freed spirit, refined through suffering and brought into divine harmony through the spirit of the living Christ, passed over the dark waters of death as on a bridge of light, over whose radiant arches hovering angels bent. They parted the dark locks from her marble brow, closed the waxen lids over the once bright and laughing eye, and left her to the dreamless slumber of the grave.

Her cousin turned from that deathbed a sadder and wiser woman. She resolved more earnestly than ever to make the world better by her example, gladder by her presence, and to kindle the fires of her genius on the altars of universal love and truth. She had a higher and better object in all her writings than the mere acquisition of gold or acquirement of fame. She felt that she had a high and holy mission on the battlefield of existence—that life was not given her to be frittered away in nonsense or wasted away in trifling pursuits. She would willingly espouse an unpopular cause, but not an unrighteous one.

In her the downtrodden slave found an earnest advocate; the flying fugitive remembered her kindness as he stepped cautiously through our Republic to gain his freedom in a monarchial land, having broken the chains on which the rust of centuries had gathered. Little children learned to name her with affection; the poor called her blessed as she broke her bread to the pale lips of hunger.

Her life was like a beautiful story, only it was clothed with the dignity of reality and invested with the sublimity of truth. True, she was an old maid; no husband brightened her life with his love or shaded it with his neglect. No children nestling lovingly in her arms called her mother. No one appended Mrs. to her name.

She was an old maid, striving to keep up an appearance of girlishness when "departed" was written on her youth, pining at her loneliness. The world was full of warm, loving hearts, and her own beat in unison with them. Neither was she always sentimentally sighing for something to love; objects of affection were all around her, and the world was not so wealthy in love that it had no use for hers. In blessing others she made a life and benediction, and as old age descended peacefully and gently upon her, she had learned one of life's most precious lessons: that true happiness consists not so much in the fruition of our wishes as in the regulation of desires and the full development and right culture of our whole natures.

Aunt Lindy

by
VICTORIA EARLE MATTHEWS

IN THE ANNALS of Fort Valley, Georgia, few events will last longer in the minds of her slow, easygoing dwellers than the memory of a great conflagration that left more than half the town a complete waste. It was generally conceded to be the most disastrous fire that even her oldest residents had ever witnessed. It was caused, as far as could be ascertained, by someone who, while passing through the sampling room of the Cotton Exchange, had thoughtlessly tossed aside a burning match; this, embedding itself in the soft fleecy cotton, burned its way silently, without smoke, through the heart of a great bale to the flooring beneath, before it was discovered.

Although the watchman made his regular rounds an hour or so after the building closed for the night, yet he saw nothing to indicate the treacherous flame which was then, like a serpent, stealing its way through the soft snowy cotton. But now a red glare, a terrified cry of "Fire! Fire!" echoing on the still night air, had aroused the unconscious sleepers and summoned quickly strong, brave-hearted men from every direction, who, as though with one accord, fell to fighting the fire-fiend (modern invention was unknown in this out-of-the-way settlement); even the women flocked to the scene, not knowing how soon a helping hand would be needed.

Great volumes of black smoke arose from the fated building, blinding and choking the stout fellows who had arranged themselves in small squads on the roofs of adjacent dwellings to check, if possible, the progress of the fire, while others in line passed water to them.

As the night wore on, a rising wind fanned the fiery tongue into a fateful blaze; and, as higher rose the wind, fiercer grew the flame; from every window and doorway poured great tongues of fire, casting a lurid glare all over the valley, with its shuddering groups of mute, frightened white faces, and its shrieking, prayerful, terror-stricken negroes, whose religion, being of a highly emotional character, was easily rendered devotional by any unusual excitement: their agonized "Almighty God! help us poor sinners," chanted in doleful tones, as only the emotional Southern negro can chant or moan, but added to the weird, wild scene. Men and women with blanched faces looked anxiously at each other; piercing screams rent the air, as some child, relative, or loved one was missed, for like a curse, the consuming fire passed from house to house, leaving nothing in its track but the blackened and charred remains of what had been, but a few short hours before, "home."

All through the night the fire raged, wasting its force as the early morning light gradually penetrated the smoky haze, revealing to the well-nigh frantic people a sad, sad scene of desolation. When home has been devastated hearts may only feel and know the extent of the void; no pen or phrase can estimate it.

As the day advanced, sickening details of the night's horror were brought to light. Magruder's Tavern, the only hotel the quaint little town could boast of, served as a death trap; several perished in the flames; many were hurt by falling beams; some jumped from windows and lay maimed for life; others stood in shuddering groups, homeless, but thankful withal that their lives had been spared: as the distressed were found, neighbors who had escaped the scourge threw wide their doors and bestirred themselves to give relief to the sufferers and temporary shelter to those who had lost all. Ah! let unbelievers cavil and contend, yet such a time as this proves that there is a mystic vein running through humanity that is not deduced from the mechanical laws of nature.

A silver-haired man, a stranger in the town, had been taken to a humble cot where many children in innocent forgetfulness passed noisily to and fro, unconscious that quiet meant life to the aged sufferer. Old Dr. Bronson, with his great heart and gentle, childlike manner, stood doubly thoughtful as he numbered the throbbing pulse. "His brain won't—can't bear it unless he's nursed and has perfect quiet," he murmured as he quitted the house. Acting upon a sudden thought, he sprang into his buggy and quickly drove through the shady lanes, by the redolent orchards, to a lone cabin on the outskirts of the town, situated at the entrance to the great sighing pine-woods.

Seeing a man weeding a small garden plot, he called, without alighting, "Hi there, Joel: where's Aunt Lindy?"

"Right there, in de cabin, doctor; jes wait a minute, as he disappeared through the doorway.

"Good day, Aunt Lindy," as a tall, ancient-looking negro dame hurried from the cabin to the gate. Well accustomed was she to these sudden calls of Dr. Bronson, for her fame as a nurse was known far beyond the limits of Fort Valley.

"Morning, doctor; Miss Martha and de children was not touched by de fire?" she inquired anxiously.

"Oh, no; the fire was not our way. Lindy, I have a bad case, and nowhere to take him. Mrs. Bronson has her hands full of distressed, suffering children. No one to nurse him, so I want to bring him here—a victim of the great fire."

"Lord, doctor, you can, you know you can; de cabin is poor, but Joel and me ain't heathens; fetch him right along my hands ain't afraid of work when trouble comes."

Tenderly they lifted him, and bore him from the cottage resounding with childish prattle and glee, to the quiet, cleanly cabin of the lonely couple, Lindy and Joel, who years before had seen babes torn from their breasts and sold—powerless to utter a complaint or appeal, whipped for the tears they shed, knowing their children would return to them not again till the graves gave up their dead But m the busy life that freedom gave them, oft, when work was done and the night of life threw its waning shadows around them, their tears would fall for the scattered voices—they would mourn over their past oppression. Yet they hid their grief from an unsympathizing generation, and the memory of their oppressors awoke but to the call of fitful retrospection.

"Joel, does you 'member what de 'scripture' says about de stranger within de gates?" asked Aunt Lindy, as she hurriedly made ready for the "victim of the great fire."

"Ole 'oman, I gits more forgitful each day I live, but it 'pears to me dat it says something 'bout 'Heal de sick an' lead the blind,' " the old man said, as he stood with a look of deep concern settling on his aged face; "yes, ole 'oman," brightening up, "yes, dat's it, 'cause I 'member de words de blessed Marster say to dem listening souls gathered 'roun him, 'If you have done it to de least of these my bredrin, you have done it onto me'."

"Yes, yes, I 'members now," Aunt Lindy murmured, as she moved the bed that the stranger was to rest upon out in the middle of the small room, the headboard near the window almost covered with climbing honeysuckle, all in sweet bloom.

"It's wonderful," she continued, meditatively, "how de Marster ranges t'ings to suit His work and will. I've kept dis bed fixed for years, 'maginin' dat somehow, in de providence of God, one of de children might chance dis way with no place to lay his head—de law me!- Joel, make haste an fetch in dat shuck bed, de sun has made it as sweet as de flowers, 'fore de dew falls off of dem, an' recollect I wants a hole parcel of mullen leaves; they're powerful good for laying fever, an' as you're going dat way you might jes as well get a handful of mounting mint, sweet balsam—an cam'ile," she called after him, "if you pass any."

About candle-light Dr. Bronson arrived with his patient, while his two assistants placed him on the bed prepared for him; the doctor explained the critical condition of the sick man to the trusty old nurse and directed as to the medicine. "Do not disturb him for an hour at least, Aunt Lindy; let him sleep, for he needs all the strength he can rally—he has but one slim chance out of ten."

"Poor soul, I'll look after him same as if he was my own chile."

"I know that, Aunt Lindy; I will stop in on my way back from the ridge in about a couple of hours."

"All right, sah."

Uncle Joel, with the desired herbs, returned shortly afterward. "Has he come yet, old 'oman?"

"Shsh! Sure nuff," she whispered, with a warning motion of her head toward the partitioned room where the sick man lay. Heeding the warning, Uncle Joel whispered back:

"If there's nothing I can do jes now to help you, I'll jes step over to Bro Anderson' s ; I hear there' s a new breddah who' s going to lead de meeting, as Bro Wilson is ailing.

"Go 'long, Joel, there's nothing you can do jes now."

"Well then, so long, ole 'oman," the old man said, as he stepped noiselessly out into the sweet perfume-laden air.

For a long time Aunt Lindy sat dozing by the smothered fire; so lightly, though, that almost the rustling of the wind through the leaves would have awakened her.

The moonlight streamed in the doorway; now and then sounds issuing from the "prayer meeting," a few doors away, could be heard on the still evening air. After a while the nurse rose, lighted a candle, and went to make sure the sick man was comfortable. Entering softly, she stepped to the bedside and looked at the face of the sleeper; suddenly she grew dizzy, breathless, amazed, as though her eyes had deceived her; she placed the candle close by his face and peered wildly at this bruised, bandaged, silver-haired stranger in a fascinated sort of way, as though she were powerless to speak. At last:

"Great God! it's Marse Jeems!"

The quick vengeful flame leaped in her eyes, as her mind, made keen by years of secret suffering and toil, traveled through time and space; she saw wrongs which no tongue can enumerate; demoniac gleams of exultation and bitter hatred settled upon her now grim features; a pitiless smile wreathed her set lips, as she gazed with glaring eyeballs at this helpless, homeless "victim of the great fire," as though surrounded by demons; a dozen wicked impulses rushed through her mind—a life for a life—no mortal eye was near, an intercepted breath, a gasp, and—

"Lindy, Lindy, don't tell Miss Cynthia,". the sick man weakly murmured: in the confused state of his brain, it required but this familiar black face to conduct his disordered thoughts to the palmiest period of his existence. He again reveled in opulence, saw again the cotton fields—a waving tract of bursting snowballs—the magnolia, the oleander—

"Where's my children?" Nurse Lindy fairly shrieked in his face. "To de four winds of de earth, you ole devil, you." He heard her not now, for white and unconscious he lay, while the long pent-up passion found vent. Her blood was afire, her tall form swayed, her long, bony hands trembled like an animal at bay; she stepped back as if to spring upon him with clutching fingers extended; breathless she paused; the shouts of the worshippers broke upon the evening air—the old-time melody seemed to pervade the cabin; she listened, turned, and fled—out through the open doorway,— out into the white moonlight, down the shadowed lane, as if impelled by unseen force. She unconsciously approached the prayer-meeting door. "Vengeance is mine, says de Lord, came from within; her anger died away; quickly her steps she retraced. "Almighty God, strengthen my arm, and purify my heart," was all she said.

Soon from the portals of death she brought him, for untiringly she labored, unceasingly she prayed in her poor broken way; nor was it in vain, for before the frost fell the crisis passed, the light of reason beamed upon the silverhaired stranger, and revealed in mystic characters the service rendered by a former slave—Aunt Lindy. He marveled at the patient faithfulness of these people. He saw but the gold—did not dream of the dross burned away by the great Refiner's fire. From that time Aunt Lindy and Uncle Joel never knew a sorrow,

66

secret or otherwise; for not only was the roof above their heads secured to them, but the new "breddah" who came to "lead de meeting in Bro Wilson's place," was proved beyond a doubt, through the efforts of the silver-haired stranger, to be their first-born. The rest were "sleeping until the morning," and not to the "four winds of de earth,"' as was so greatly feared by Aunt Lindy.

Black Is, As Black Does (A Dream)

by
ANGELINA W. GRIMKE

IT CAME TO ME one dark, rainy morning as I was half awake and half asleep. The wind was blowing drearily, and I listened to the swish of the rain upon the glass and the dripping from the eaves. As I lay listening I thought many things, and my thoughts grew hazier and hazier, and I fell into deep slumber.

Then a great feeling of peace came upon me and that all my cares were falling from me and rolling away — away into infinity. As I lay with my eyes closed, this great feeling of peace increased, and my heart was glad within me. Then someone touched me lightly upon the shoulder and eyes, causing my heart to give a great bound, for I was not prepared for the loveliness of the scene which now burst upon my sight. Stretched all around was a wide, green, grassy plain. Each little blade of grass sang in the gentle wind, and here and there massive trees spread their branches. The leaves and the birds made music, while the river passing through the meadow sparkled and sang as it sped on its way. Listening, I heard no discord, for all the voices blended with each other, mingling and swelling and making one grand sweet song. I longed to sing too, and I lifted up my voice, but no song came, so that I wondered. Then a voice at my side answered: "Thou art not one of us yet." The voice was sweeter than the babbling brook, more tender than the voice of a mother to her erring child, lower than the beating of the restless surf on the shore. Then I turned to see whence this voice came. As I looked I fell upon my face weeping.

For there stood before me a figure clad in white. As she moved she seemed like a snowy-white cloud, which sails over the sky in summertime. A soft light shone above, around, behind, illuminating her.

It was not for this I fell to weeping. I had looked upon the face, and the truth which shone forth from the mild eyes, the sweetness which smiled around the mouth, and all the pity, the mercy, the kindness, expressed in that divine countenance, revealed to me how wicked I was, and had been. But she took me by the hand, bidding me arise, and kissed me on the brow. Between my sobs I asked: "Where am l?" The low voice answered: "This is heaven." I said: "Who art thou?" She answered: "One of the lovers of Cod." And as she spoke that name, the heavens brightened, the grass sang sweeter, as did the leaves and the birds, also the silvery river. Looking up, I saw that she was no longer by my side, but was moving over the plain, and turning, she beckoned to me. I followed without knowing why.

Thus we passed silently over the velvety grass, over hill and dale, by laughing brooks and swift-flowing rivers. Often turning, she smiled upon me, but on and on we went; now and then other bright spirits passed us, all smiling kindly upon me as they went their way. Some came and kissed my forehead and said they were glad to see me, and I was happy, *so* happy. Then we came to a city, but ah! so unlike our cities: no hurrying this and that way, no deafening roar of passing wagons, no shrieking hucksters, no loud talking, no anxious, worried faces. All was peace. And as we passed up the noiseless streets, many spirits clad in spotless white, and gleaming with that ineffable light, passed, and all smiled and greeted me tenderly as they went their shining way.

Then we came to a great hall. The doors thereby were three and opened wide, and I saw many people going in through the first door, but they were not clad in snowy white, and I could see no light illuminating their bodies. I asked: Pray tell me who are these?" And the spirit said: These are those, like you, who have just come from earth. And as she spoke, I saw some passing forth from the second door, dad in white, but I saw no light, and I said perplexed: "Pray who are these, and why does no light illuminate them?" She answered: "These are they whom our *Father* has blessed of those who have just come from earth, and they will have the light when they have been with us a long time, when they have done some service which has particularly gratified *our Father*. "' She had scarcely ceased speaking when I saw several ragged ones, with looks downcast, coming through the third door; and I asked: "Pray who are these?" As she answered, her voice trembled, and gazing upon her, I saw a tear glide down her cheek as she answered, simply: "The lost." And, groaning within me I said: "Pray what is this place?" And solemnly she answered: "This is where God weeds out the wicked from the good." And as she ceased speaking, she glided to the first door and beckoned me.

We came within a hall, large and gloomy, and we passed down one end, and looking up, I saw a great, dazzling light, that was all; for I fell upon the floor, overcome. I had looked upon *God*! As I lay I heard his voice now low and tender beyond expression, now stern and mighty, like the roll of thunder. When I took courage I gazed around, but I dared not look upon *His* face again.

I saw a vast multitude of those lately come from earth, waiting to stand before the bar of judgment; also those who had been tried, passing out through the doors. Looking at my companion, I saw that she was gazing upon *God*, and His brightness shone upon her face, and I was dazzled and looked down. When I glanced upon the throng of the lately dead, I saw one pass to the bar and fall with a loud cry for mercy. I heard him weeping and confessing all his sins, excusing himself in nothing, and I saw that his skin was black; looking closer, I saw that he was lame, torn, and bleeding, and quite unrecognizable, for most of his features were gone. I saw him waving his poor stumps of arms, begging for mercy. By these tokens I knew that he came from my country, and that he was one of an oppressed race; for in America, alas! it makes a difference whether a man's *skin* be black or white. Nothing was said, but I perceived that he had been foully murdered.

I heard *God's* voice speaking to him, and I was lost in its sweetness. It seemed to me I was floating down a stream of loveliness, and I was so happy. When He ceased, I thought I had gently come to some bank, and all was peace and rest. And I saw the man pass from the bar, and that he was clad in pure white. Beautiful spirits came and tended his wounds, and lo! he stood forth glorified, a dim light shining round him. I looked at my companion and she smiled, and then I understood. And behold another stood before the *Judgment-seat* I did not hear *him* beg for mercy, but I heard him telling all the good he had done, and I heard a sound as of distant mutterings of thunder, and I felt the angry flashings above the *Judgment-seat*. And I saw the man waiting calmly in his own conceit. And I heard the muffled thunder of God's voice asking: "And didst thou treat all my children justly?" And I heard the man say: "Yea, yea, O Lord!" And I heard God again: "Whether their skin was black or white?" And the man answered: "Yea, yea, Lord, and laughed.

Then I heard the thunder of God's voice saying: "I know thee, who thou art; it was thou who didst murder yon man, one of my faithful servants; it was thou who didst hate and torture him, and who trampled upon and crushed him; but inasmuch as thou didst this wrong unto him, thou didst it unto me. Begone!" And I saw him who was condemned stagger from the bar, and that his hands and his clothes were covered with blood, and that he left behind him footprints tracked in blood; and as I looked at him more closely, I saw that his skin was white, but that his *soul* was black. For it makes a difference in heaven whether a man's *soul* be black or white!

And I beheld the man with the black skin creep up to the *Judgment -seat* and sob, brokenly: "Forgive, oh, forgive my brother, for he knew not what he did." And I felt my heart beating and tumbling against my side—and I awoke. The wind was moaning drearily, the rain was still sobbing against the glass, and I lay there and wept.

The Stones of the Village

by
ALICE DUNBAR-NELSON

VICTOR GRABERT STRODE down the one, wide, tree-shaded street of the village, his heart throbbing with a bitterness and anger that seemed too great to bear. So often had he gone home in the same spirit, however, that it had grown nearly second nature to him—this dull, sullen resentment, flaming out now and then into almost murderous vindictiveness. Behind him there floated derisive laughs and shouts, the taunts of little brutes, boys of his own age.

He reached the tumbledown cottage at the farther end of the street and flung himself on the battered step. Grandmere Grabért sat rocking herself to and fro, crooning a bit of song brought over from the West Indies years ago; but when the boy sat silent, his head bowed in his hands, she paused in the midst of a line and regarded him with keen, piercing eyes.

"Eh, Victor?" she asked. That was all, but he understood. He raised his head and waved a hand angrily down the street toward the lighted square that marked the village center.

"Those boys," he gulped.

Grandmere Grabért laid a sympathetic hand on his black curls, but withdrew it the next instant.

"*Bien*, " she said angrily. "Why d'you go by dem, eh? Why not keep to yourself? They don't want you, they don't care for you. Ain't' you got no sense?"

"Oh, but Grandmere," he wailed piteously, "I want to play."

The old woman stood up in the doorway, her tall, spare form towering menacingly over him.

"You want to play, eh? Why? You don't need no play. Dose boy"—she swept a magnificent gesture down the street—"they're fools!"

72

"If I could play with—" began Victor, but his grandmother caught him by the wrist and held him as in a vise.

Hush," she cried. "You must be goin' crazy." And still holding him by the wrist, she pulled him indoors.

It was a two-room house, bare and poor and miserable, but never had it seemed so meager before to Victor as it did this night. The supper was frugal almost to the starvation point. They ate in silence, and afterward Victor threw himself on his cot in the corner of the kitchen and closed his eyes. Grandmere Grabért thought him asleep and closed the door noiselessly as she went into her own room But he was awake, and his mind was like a shifting kaleidoscope of miserable incidents and heartaches. He had lived fourteen years, and he could remember most of them as years of misery. He had never known a mother's love, for his mother had died, so he was told, when he was but a few months old. No one ever spoke to him of a father, and Grandmere Grabért had been all to him. She was kind, after a stern, unloving fashion, and she provided for him as best she could. He had picked up some sort of an education at the parish school. It was a good one after its way, but his life there had been such a succession of miseries that he rebelled one day and refused to go anymore.

His earliest memories were clustered about this poor little cottage. He could see himself toddling about its broken steps, playing alone with a few broken pieces of china which his fancy magnified into glorious toys. He remembered his first whipping too. Tired one day of the loneliness which even the broken china could not mitigate, he had toddled out the side gate after a merry group of little black and yellow boys of his own age. When Grandmere Grabért, missing him from his accustomed garden corner, came to look for him, she found him sitting contentedly in the center of the group in the dusty street, all of them gravely scooping up handfuls of the gravelly dirt and trickling it down their chubby bare legs. Grandmere snatched at him fiercely, and he whimpered, for he was learning for the first time what fear was.

"What you mean?" she hissed at him. "What you mean playin' in de street with those niggers?" And she struck at him wildly with her open hand.

He looked up into her brown face surmounted by a wealth of curly black hair faintly streaked with gray, but he was too frightened to question.

It had been loneliness ever since. For the parents of the little black and yellow boys, resenting the insult Grandmere had offered their

73

offspring, sternly bade them have nothing more to do with Victor. Then when he toddled after some other little boys, whose faces were white like his own, they ran him away with derisive hoots of "Nigger! Nigger!" And again, he could not understand.

Hardest of all, though, was when Grandmere sternly bade him cease speaking the soft Creole patois that they chattered together and forced him to learn English. The result was a confused jumble which was no language at all; that when he spoke it in the streets or in the school, all the boys, white and black and yellow, hooted at him and called him "White nigger! White nigger!"

He writhed on his cot that night and lived over all the anguish of his years until hot tears scalded their way down a burning face, and he fell into a troubled sleep wherein he sobbed over some dreamland miseries

The next morning, Grandmere eyed his heavy swollen eyes sharply, and a momentary thrill of compassion passed over her and found expression in a new tenderness of manner toward him as she served his breakfast. She, too, had thought over the matter in the night, and it bore fruit in an unexpected way.

Some few weeks after, Victor found himself timidly ringing the doorbell of a house on Hospital Street in New Orleans. His heart throbbed in painful unison to the jangle of the bell. How was he to know that old Madame Guichard, Grandmere's one friend in the city, to whom she had confided him, would be kind? He had walked from the river landing to the house, timidly inquiring the way of busy pedestrians. He was hungry and frightened. Never in all his life had he seen so many people before, and in all the busy streets there was not one eye which would light up with recognition when it met his own. Moreover, it had been a weary journey down the Red River, thence into the Mississippi, and finally here. Perhaps it had not been devoid of interest, after its fashion, but Victor did not know. He was too heartsick at leaving home.

However, Madame Guichard was kind. She welcomed him with a volubility and overflow of tenderness that acted like balm to the boy's sore spirit. Thence they were firm friends, even confidants.

Victor must find work to do. Grandmere Grabért's idea in sending him to New Orleans was that he might "mek one man of himself," as she phrased it. And Victor, grown suddenly old m the sense that he had a responsibility to bear, set about his search valiantly.

It chanced one day that he saw a sign in an old bookstore on Royal Street that stated in both French and English the need of a boy.

Almost before he knew it, he had entered the shop and was gasping out some choked words to the little old man who sat behind the counter.

The old man looked keenly over his glasses at the boy and rubbed his bald head reflectively. In order to do this, he had to take off an old black silk cap, which he looked at with apparent regret.

"Eh, what you say?" he asked sharply, when Victor had finished.

"I—I—want a place to work," stammered the boy again.

"Eh, you do? Well, can you read?"

"Yes sir," replied Victor.

The old man got down from his stool, came from behind the counter, and putting his finger under the boy's chin, stared hard into his eyes. They met his own unflinchingly, though there was the suspicion of pathos and timidity in their brown depths.

"Do you know where you live, eh?"

"On Hospital Street," said Victor. It did not occur to him to give the number, and the old man did not ask.

"*Tres bien*," grunted the book-seller, and his interest relaxed. He gave a few curt directions about the manner of work Victor was to do and settled himself again upon his stool, poring into his dingy book with renewed ardor.

Thus began Victor's commercial life. It was an easy one. At seven, he opened the shutters of the little shop and swept and dusted. At eight, the book-seller came down stairs and passed out to get his coffee at the restaurant across the street. At eight in the evening, the shop was closed again. That was all.

Occasionally, there came a customer, but not often, for there were only odd books and rare ones in the shop, and those who came were usually old, yellow, querulous bookworms, who nosed about for hours and went away leaving many bank notes behind them. Sometimes there was an errand to do, and sometimes there came a customer when the proprietor was out. It was an easy matter to wait on them. He had but to point to the shelves and say, "Monsieur will be in directly," and all was settled, for those who came here to buy had plenty of leisure and did not mind waiting.

So a year went by, then two and three, and the stream of Victor's life flowed smoothly on its uneventful way. He had grown tall and thin, and often Madame Guichard would look at him and chuckle to herself, "Ha, he is like a beanpole, yes, *mais*—" and there would be a world of unfinished reflection in that last word.

Victor had grown pale from much reading. Like a shadow of the old book-seller he sat day after day poring into some dusty yellow-paged book, and his mind was a queer jumble of ideas. History and philosophy and old-fashioned social economy were tangled with French romance and classic mythology and astrology and mysticism He had made few friends, for his experience in the village had made him chary of strangers. Every week, he wrote to Grandmere Grabért and sent her part of his earnings. In his way he was happy, and if he was lonely, he had ceased to care about it, for his world was peopled with images of his own fancying.

Then all at once, the world he had built about him tumbled down, and he was left, staring helplessly at its ruins. The little book-seller died one day, and his shop and its books were sold by an unscrupulous nephew who cared not for bindings nor precious yellowed pages, but only for the grossly material things that money can buy. Victor ground his teeth as the auctioneer's strident voice sounded through the shop where all once had been hushed quiet, and wept as he saw some of his favorite books carried away by men and women who he was sure could not appreciate their value.

He dried his tears, however, the next day, when a grave-faced lawyer came to the little house on Hospital Street and informed him that he had been left a sum of money by the book-seller.

Victor sat staring at him helplessly. Money meant little to him. He never needed it, never used it. After he had sent Grandmere her sum each week Madame Guichard kept the rest and doled it out to him as he needed it for carfare and clothes.

"The interest of the money," continued the lawyer clearing his throat, "is sufficient to keep you very handsomely without touching the principal. It was my client's wish that you should enter Tulane College and there fit yourself for your profession. He had great confidence in your ability."

"Tulane College!" cried Victor. "Why—why—why—" Then he stopped suddenly, and the hot blood mounted to his face. He glanced furtively about the room. Madame Guichard was not near; the lawyer had seen no one but him. Then why tell him? His heart leaped wildly at the thought. Well, Grandmere would have willed it so.

The lawyer was waiting politely for him to finish his sentence.

"Why—why—I should have to study in order to enter there," finished Victor lamely.

"Exactly so," said Mr. Buckley, "and as I have, in a way, been appointed your guardian, I will see to that."

Victor found himself murmuring confused thanks and good-byes

76

to Mr. Buckley. After he had gone, the boy sat down and gazed blankly at the wall. Then he wrote a long letter to Grandmere.

A week later, he changed boarding places at Mr. Buckley's advice and entered a preparatory school for Tulane. And still, Madame Guichard and Mr. Buckley had not met.

It was a handsomely furnished office on Carondelet Street in which Lawyer Grabért sat some years later. His day's work done, he was leaning back in his chair and smiling pleasantly out of the window. Within was warmth and light and cheer; without, the wind howled and gusty rains beat against the window pane. Lawyer Grabért smiled again as he looked about at the comfort and found himself half pitying those without who were forced to buffet the storm afoot. He rose finally and, donning his overcoat, called a cab and was driven to his rooms in the most fashionable part of the city. There he found his old-time college friend, awaiting him with some impatience.

"Thought you never were coming, old man," was his greeting.

Grabért smiled pleasantly, "Well, I was a bit tired, you know," he answered, "and I have been sitting idle for an hour or more, just relaxing, as it were."

Vannier laid his hand affectionately on the other's shoulder. "That was a mighty effort you made today," he said earnestly. "I, for one, am proud of you "

"Thank you," replied Grabért simply, and the two sat silent for a minute.

"Going to the Charles' dance tonight?" asked Vannier finally.

"I don't believe I am. I am tired and lazy."

"It will do you good. Come on."

"No, I want to read and ruminate."

"Ruminate over your good fortune of today?"

"If you will have it so, yes."

But it must not simply over his good fortune of that day over which Grabért pondered. It was over the good fortune of the past fifteen years. From school to college, and from college to law school he had gone, and thence into practice, and he was now accredited a successful young lawyer. His small fortune, which Mr. Buckley, with generous kindness had invested wisely, had almost doubled, and his school career, while not of the brilliant, meteoric kind, had been pleasant and profitable. He had made friends, at first, with the boys he met, and they in turn had taken him into their homes. Now and then, the Buckleys asked him to dinner, and he was seen occasionally in their box at the opera. He was rapidly becoming a social favorite, and girls vied with each other to dance with him. No one had asked any questions, and he had volunteered no information concerning himself. Vannier, who had known him in preparatory school days, had said that he was a young country fellow with some money, no connections, and a ward of Mr. Buckley s, and somehow, contrary to the usual social custom of the South, this meager account had passed muster. But Vannier s family had been a social arbiter for many years, and Grabért s personality was pleasing without being aggressive, so he had passed through the portals of the social world and was in the inner circle.

One year, when he and Vannier were in Switzerland, pretending to climb impossible mountains and in reality smoking many cigars a day on hotel porches, a letter came to Grabért from the priest of his old-time town, telling him that Grandmere Grabért had been laid away in the parish churchyard. There was no more to tell. The little old hut had been sold to pay funeral expenses.

"Poor Grandmere," sighed Victor. "She did care for me after her fashion. I'll go take a look at her grave when I go back."

But he did not go, for when he returned to Louisiana, he was too busy, then he decided that it would be useless, sentimental folly. Moreover, he had no love for the old village. Its very name suggested things that made him turn and look about him nervously. He had long since eliminated Madame Guichard from his list of acquaintances.

And yet, as he sat there in his cozy study that night and smiled as he went over in his mind triumph after triumph which he had made since the old bookstore days in Royal Street, he was conscious of a subtle undercurrent of annoyance; a sort of mental reservation that placed itself on every pleasant memory.

"I wonder what's the matter with me?" he asked himself as he rose and paced the floor impatiently. Then he tried to recall his other triumph, the one of the day. The case of Tate vs. Tate, a famous will contest, had been dragging through the courts for seven years, and his speech had decided it that day. He could hear the applause of the courtroom as he sat down, but it rang hollow in his ears, for he remembered another scene. The day before he had been in another court and found himself interested in the prisoner before the bar. The offense was a slight one, a mere technicality. Grabért was conscious of a something pleasant in the man's face; a scrupulous neatness in his dress, an unostentatious conforming to the prevailing style. The Recorder, however, was short and brusque.

"Wilson—Wilson—" he growled. "Oh, yes, I know you, always kicking up some sort of a row about theater seats and cars. Hum-um. What do you mean by coming before me with a flower in your buttonhole?"

The prisoner looked down indifferently at the bud on his coat and made no reply.

"Hey?" growled the Recorder. "You niggers are putting yourselves up too much for me."

At the forbidden word, the blood rushed to Grabért's face, and he started from his seat angrily. The next instant he had recovered himself and buried his face in a paper After Wilson had paid his fine, Grabért looked at him furtively as he passed out. His face was perfectly impassive, but his eyes flashed defiantly. The lawyer was tingling with rage and indignation, although the affront had not been given him.

"If Recorder Grant had any reason to think that I was in any way like Wilson, I would stand no better show," he mused bitterly.

However, as he thought it over tonight, he decided that he was a sentimental fool. "What have I to do with them" he asked himself. "I must be careful."

The next week he discharged the man who cared for his office. He was a Negro, and Grabért had no fault to find with him generally, but he found himself with a growing sympathy toward the man, and since the episode in the courtroom, he was morbidly nervous lest a something in his manner would betray him. Thereafter, a round-eyed Irish boy cared for his rooms

The Vanniers were wont to smile indulgently at his every move. Elise Vannier particularly was more than interested in his work. He had a way of dropping in of evenings and talking over his cases and speeches with her in a cozy corner of the library. She had a gracious sympathetic manner that was soothing and a cheery fund of repartee to whet her conversation. Victor found himself drifting into sentimental bits of talk now and then. He found himself carrying around in his pocketbook a faded rose which she had once worn, and when he laughed at it one day and started to throw it in the wastebasket, he suddenly kissed it instead and replaced it in the pocketbook. That Elise was not indifferent to him he could easily see. She had not learned yet how to veil her eyes and mask her face under a cool assumption of superiority. She would give him her hand, when they met, with a girlish impulsiveness, and her color came and went under his gaze. Sometimes, when he held her hand a bit longer than necessary, he could feel it flutter in his own, and she would sigh a quick little gasp that made his heart leap and choked his utterance.

They were tucked away in their usual cozy corner one evening, and the conversation had drifted to the problem of where they would spend the summer.

"Papa wants to go to the country house," pouted Elise, "and Mama and I don't want to go. It isn't fair, of course, because when we go so far away, Papa can be with us only for a few weeks when he can get away from his office, while if we go to the country place, he can run up every few days. But it is so dull there, don't you think so?"

Victor recalled some pleasant vacation days at the plantation home and laughed. "Not if you are there."

"Yes, but you see, I can't take myself for a companion. Now if you'll promise to come up sometimes, it will be better."

"If I may, I shall be delighted to come."

Elise laughed intimately. "If you may— she replied. "As if such a word had to enter into our plans. Oh, but Victor, haven't you some sort of plantation somewhere? It seems to me that I heard Steven years ago speak of your home in the country, and I wondered sometimes that you never spoke of it or ever mentioned having visited it.

The girl's artless words were bringing cold sweat to Victor's brow, his tongue felt heavy and useless, but he managed to answer quietly, "I have no home in the country."

"Well, didn't you ever own one, or your family?"

"It was old quite a good many years ago," he replied, and a vision of the little old hut with its tumbledown steps and weed-grown garden came into his mind.

"Where was it?" pursued Elise innocently.

"Oh, away up in St. Landry parish, too far away from civilization to mention." He tried to laugh, but it was a hollow forced attempt that rang false. But Elise was too absorbed in her own thoughts of the summer to notice.

"And you haven't a relative living?" she continued.

"Not one."

"How strange. Why, it seems to me if I did not have a half a hundred cousins and uncles and aunts that I should feel somehow out of touch with the world."

He did not reply, and she chattered away on another topic.

When he was alone in his room that night, he paced the floor

80

again, chewing wildly at a cigar that he had forgotten to light.

"What did she mean? What did she mean?" he asked himself over and over. Could she have heard or suspected anything that she was trying to find out about? Could any action, any unguarded expression of his, have set the family thinking? But he soon dismissed the thought as unworthy of him. Elise was too frank and transparent a girl to stoop to subterfuge. If she wished to know anything, she was wont to ask out at once, and if she had once thought anyone was sailing under false colors, she would say so frankly and dismiss them from her presence.

Well, he must be prepared to answer questions if he were going to marry her. The family would want to know all about him, and Elise, herself, would be curious for more than her brother Steve Vannier's meager account. But was he going to marry Elise? That was the question.

He sat down and buried his head in his hands. Would it be right for him to take a wife, especially such a woman as Elise, and from such a family as the Vanniers? Would it be fair? Would it be just? If they knew and were willing, it would be different. But they did not know, and they would not consent if they did. In fancy, he saw the dainty girl whom he loved shrinking from him as he told her of Grandmere Grabért and the village boys. This last thought made him set his teeth hard, and the hot blood rushed to his face.

Well, why not, after all, why not? What was the difference between him and the hosts of other suitors who hovered about Elise? They had money;. so had he. They had education, polite training, culture, social position; so had he. But they had family traditions, and he had none. Most of them could point to a long line of family portraits with justifiable pride; while if he had had a picture of Grandmere Grabért, he would have destroyed it fearfully, lest it fall into the hands of some too curious person. This was the subtle barrier that separated them. He recalled with a sting how often he had had to sit silent and constrained when the conversation turned to ancestors and family traditions. He might be one with his companions and friends in everything but this. He must ever be on the outside, hovering at the gates, as it were. Into the inner life of his social world, he might never enter. The charming impoliteness of an intercourse begun by their fathers and grandfathers was not for him. There must always be a certain formality with him, even though they were his most intimate friends. He had not fifty cousins, therefore, as Elise phrased it, he was "out of touch with the world."

"If ever I have a son or a daughter," he found himself saying unconsciously, "I would try to save him from this."

Then he laughed bitterly as he realized the irony of the thought. Well, anyway, Elise loved him. There was a sweet consolation in that. He had but to look into her frank eyes and read her soul. Perhaps she wondered why he had not spoken. Should he speak? There he was back at the old question again.

"According to the standard of the world," he mused reflectively, "my blood is tainted in two ways. Who knows it? No one but myself, and I shall not tell. Otherwise, I am quite as good as the rest, and Elise loves me."

But even this thought failed of its sweetness in a moment. Elise loved him because she did not know. He found a sickening anger and disgust rising in himself at a people whose prejudices made him live a life of deception. He would cater to their traditions no longer; he would be honest. Then he found himself shrinking from the alternative with a dread that made him wonder. It was the old problem of his life in the village; and the boys, both white and black and yellow, stood as before, with stones in their hands to hurl at him.

He went to bed worn out with the struggle, but still with no definite idea what to do. Sleep was impossible. He rolled and tossed miserably and cursed the fate that had thrown him in such a position. He had never thought very seriously over the subject before. He had rather drifted with the tide and accepted what came to him as a sort of recompense the world owed him for his unhappy childhood. He had known fear, yes, and qualms now and then, and a hot resentment occasionally when the outsideness of his situation was inborne to him; but that was all. Elise had awakened a disagreeable conscientiousness within him, which he decided was as unpleasant as it was unnecessary.

He could not sleep, so he arose, and dressing, walked out and stood on the banquette. The low hum of the city came to him like the droning of some sleepy insect, and ever and anon, the quick flash and fire of the gas houses like a huge winking fiery eye lit up the south of the city. It was inexpressingly soothing to Victor; the great unknowing city, teeming with life and with lives whose sadness mocked his own teacup tempest. He smiled and shook himself as a dog shakes off the water from his coat

"I think a walk will help me out;" he said absently, and presently he was striding down St. Charles Avenue, around Lee Circle and down to Canal Street, where the lights and glare absorbed him for a while. He walked out the wide boulevard toward Claiborne Street, hardly thinking, hardly realizing that he was walking. When he was thoroughly worn out, he retraced his steps and dropped wearily into a restaurant near Bourbon Street.

"Hullo!" said a familiar voice from a table as he entered. Victor turned and recognized Frank Ward, a little oculist, whose office was in the same building as his own.

"Another night owl besides myself," laughed Ward, making room for him at his table. "Can't you sleep too, old fellow?"

"Not very well," said Victor taking the proferred seat. "I believe I'm getting nerves. Think I need toning up."

"Well, you'd have been toned up if you had been in here a few minutes ago. Why—why—" and Ward went off into peals of laughter at the memory of the scene.

"What was it?" asked Victor.

"Why—a fellow came in here, nice sort of fellow, apparently, and wanted to have supper. Well, would you believe it, when they wouldn't serve him, he wanted to fight everything in sight. It was positively exciting for a time.

"Why wouldn't the waiter serve him?" Victor tried to make his tone indifferent, but he felt the quaver in his voice.

"Why? Why, he was a darkey, you know."

"Well; what of it?" demanded Grabért fiercely. "Wasn't he quiet, well-dressed, polite? Didn't he have money?

"My dear fellow," began Ward mockingly. "Upon my word, I believe you are losing your mind. You do need toning up or something. Would you—could you—?

"Oh, pshaw," broke in Grabért. "I—I—believe I am losing my mind. Really, Ward, I need something to make me sleep. My head aches."

Ward was at once all sympathy and advice, and chiding to the waiter for his slowness in filling their order. Victor toyed with his food and made an excuse to leave the restaurant as soon as he could decently.

"Good heavens," he said when he was alone. "What will I do next?" His outburst of indignation at Ward's narrative had come from his lips almost before he knew it, and he was frightened, frightened at his own unguardedness. He did not know what had come over him.

"I must be careful, I must be careful," he muttered to himself. "I must go to the other extreme, if necessary." He was pacing his rooms

83

again, and suddenly, he faced the mirror.

"You wouldn't fare any better than the rest, if they knew," he told the reflection. "You poor wretch, what are you?"

When he thought of Elise, he smiled. He loved her, but he hated the traditions which she represented. He was conscious of a blind fury which bade him wreak vengeance on those traditions, and of a cowardly fear which cried out to him to retain his position in the world's and Elise's eyes at any cost.

Mrs. Grabért was delighted to have visiting her her old school friend from Virginia, and the two spent hours laughing over their girlish escapades, and comparing notes about their little ones. Each was confident that her darling had said the cutest things, and their polite deference to each other's opinions on the matter was a sham through which each saw without resentment.

"But Elise," remonstrated Mrs. Allen, "I think it so strange you don't have a mammy for Baby Vannier. He would be so much better cared for than by that harumscarum young white girl you have."

"I think so too, Adelaide," sighed Mrs. Grabért. "It seems strange for me not to have a darkey maid about, but Victor can't bear them. I cried and cried for my old mammy, but he was stern. He doesn't like darkeys, you know, and he says old mammies just frighten children and ruin their childhood. I don't see how he could say that, do you? She looked wistfully to Mrs. Allen for sympathy.

I don't know," mused that lady. "We were all looked after by our mammies, and I think they are the best kind of nurses."

"And Victor won't have any kind of darkey servant either here or at the office. He says they're shiftless and worthless and generally no-account. Of course, he knows, he's had lots of experience with them in his business."

Mrs. Allen folded her hands behind her head and stared hard at the ceiling. "Oh, well, men don't know everything," she said, "and Victor may come around to our way of thinking after all."

It was late that evening when the lawyer came in for dinner. His eyes had acquired a habit of veiling themselves under their lashes as if they were constantly concealing something which they feared might be wrenched from them by a stare. He was nervous and restless, with a habit of glancing about him furtively, and a twitching compressing of his lips when he had finished a sentence, which somehow reminded you of a kindhearted judge who is forced to give a death sentence.

Elise met him at the door as was her wont, and she knew from the first glance into his eyes that something had disturbed him more than usual that day, but she forbore asking questions, for she knew he would tell her when the time had come.

They were in their room that night when the rest of the household lay in slumber. He sat for a long while gazing at the open fire, then he passed his hand over his forehead wearily.

"I have had a rather unpleasant experience today, he began.

"Yes."

"Pavageau, again."

His wife was brushing her hair before the mirror. At the name she turned hastily with the brush in her uplifted hand.

"I can't understand, Victor, why you must have dealings with that man. He is constantly irritating you. I simply wouldn't associate with him."

"I don't," and he laughed at her feminine argument. It isn't a question of association, *chérie*, it's a purely business and unsocial relation, if relation it may be called, that throws us together."

She threw down the brush petulantly and came to his side. "Victor," she began hesitatingly, her arms about his neck, her face close to his, "won't you—won't you give up politics for me? It was ever so much nicer when you were just a lawyer and wanted only to be the best lawyer in the state, without all this worry about corruption and votes and such things. You've changed, oh, Victor, you've changed so. Baby and I won't know you after a while."

He put her gently on his knee. "You musn't blame the poor politics, darling. Don't you think, perhaps, it's the inevitable hardening and embittering that must come to us all as we grow older?"

"No, I don't," she replied emphatically. "Why do you go into this struggle, anyhow? You have nothing to gain but an empty honor. It won't bring you more money, or make you more loved or respected. Why must you be mixed up with such—such—awful people?"

"I don't know," he said wearily.

And in truth, he did not know. He had gone on after his marriage with Elise making one success after another. It seemed that a beneficent Providence had singled him out as the one man in the state upon whom to heap the most lavish attentions. He was popular after the fashion of those who are high in the esteem of the world; and this very fact made him tremble the more, for he feared that should some disclosure come, he could not stand the shock of public opinion that must overwhelm him.

"What disclosure?" he would say impatiently when such a thought would come to him. "Where could it come from, and then, what is there to disclose?"

Thus he would deceive himself for as much as a month at

He was surprised to find awaiting him in his office one day the man Wilson, whom he remembered in the courtroom before Recorder Grant. He was surprised and annoyed. Why had the man come to his office? Had he seen the telltale flush on his face that day?

But it was soon evident that Wilson did not even remember having seen him before

"I came to see if I could retain you in a case of mine," he began, after the usual formalities of greeting were over.

I am afraid, my good man," said Grabért brusquely that you have mistaken the office."

Wilson's face flushed at the appellation, but he went on bravely. I have not mistaken the office. I know you are the best civil lawyer in the city, and I want your services."

An impossible thing."

"Why? Are you too busy? My case is a simple thing, a mere point in law, but I want the best authority and the best opinion brought to bear on it."

"I could not give you any help—and—I fear, we do not understand each other—I do not wish to." He turned to his desk abruptly.

"What could he have meant by coming to me? he questioned himself fearfully, as Wilson left the office. "Do I look like a man likely to take up his impossible contentions?"

He did not look like it, nor was he. When it came to a question involving the Negro, Victor Grabért was noted for his stern, unrelenting attitude; it was simply impossible to convince him that there was anything but sheerest incapacity in that race. For him, no good could come out of this Nazareth. He was liked and respected by men of his political belief, because, even when he was a candidate for a judgeship, neither money nor the possible chance of a deluge of votes from the First and Fourth Wards could cause him to swerve one hair's breadth from his opinion of the black inhabitants of those wards.

Pavageau, however, was his *bete noir*. Pavageau was a lawyer, a coolheaded, calculating man with steely eyes set in a grim brown face. They had first met in the courtroom in a case which involved the question whether a man may set aside the will of his father who, disregarding the legal offspring of another race than himself, chooses to leave his property to educational institutions which would not have granted admission to that son. Pavageau represented the son. He lost, of course. The judge, the jury, the people, and Grabért were against him; but he fought his fight with a grim determination which commanded Victor's admiration and respect.

"Fools," he said between his teeth to himself, when they were crowding about him with congratulations. "Fools, can't they see who is the abler man of the two?"

He wanted to go up to Pavageau and give him his hand; to tell him that he was proud of him and that he had really won the case, but public opinion was against him; but he dared not. Another one of his colleagues might; but he was afraid. Pavageau and the world might misunderstand, or would it be understanding?

Thereafter they met often. Either by some freak of nature, or because there was a shrewd sense of the possibilities in his position, Pavageau was of the same political side of the fence as Grabért. Secretly, he admired the man; he respected him; he liked him, and because of this he was always ready with sneer and invective for him. He fought him bitterly when there was no occasion for fighting, and Pavageau became his enemy, and his name a very synonym of horror to Elise, who learned to trace her husband s fits of moodiness and depression to the one source.

Meanwhile, Vannier Grabért was growing up, a handsome lad, with his father s and mother s physical beauty, and a strength and force of character that belonged to neither. In him, Grabért saw the reparation of all his childhood's wrongs and sufferings. The boy realized all his own longings. He had family traditions, and a social position which was his from birth and an inalienable right to hold up his head without an unknown fear gripping at his heart. Grabért felt that he could forgive all; the village boys of long ago, and the imaginary village boys of today when he looked at his son. He had bought and paid for Vannier s freedom and happiness. The coins may have been each a drop of his hearts blood, but he had reckoned the cost before he had given it.

It was a source of great pride for him to take the boy to court with him, now that he was a judge, and one Saturday morning when he was starting out, Vannier asked if he might go.

There is nothing that would interest you today, *mon fils*," he said tenderly, "but you may go."

In fact, there was nothing interesting that day; merely a trouble-some old woman, who instead of taking her fair-skinned grandchild out of the school, where it had been found it did not belong, had pre-ferred to bring the matter to court. She was represented by Pavageau. Of course, there was not the ghost of a show for her. Pavageau had told her that. The law was very explicit about the matter. The only question lay in proving the child s affinity to the Negro race, which was not such a difficult matter to do, so the case was quickly settled, since the child s grandmother accompanied him. The judge, howev-er, was irritated. It was a hot day, and he was provoked that such a trivial matter should have taken up his time. He lost his temper as he looked at his watch.

I don't see why these people want to force their children into the white schools, he declared. There should be a rigid inspection to pre-vent it, and all the suspected children put out and made to go where they belong.

Pavageau, too, was irritated that day. He looked up from some papers which he was folding, and his gaze met Grabért s with a keen, cold, penetrating flash.

"Perhaps Your Honor would like to set the example by taking your son from the schools."

There was an instant silence in the courtroom, a hush intense and eager. Every eye turned upon the judge, who sat still, a figure carved in stone with livid face and fear-stricken eyes. After the first flash of his eyes, Pavageau had gone on coolly sorting the papers.

The courtroom waited, waited, for the judge to rise and thunder forth a fine against the daring Negro lawyer for contempt. A minute passed, which seemed like an hour. Why did not Grabért speak? Pavageau s implied accusation was too absurd for denial; but he should be punished. Was His Honor ill, or did he merely hold the man in too much contempt to notice him or his remark?

Finally Grabért spoke; he moistened his lips, for they were dry and parched, and his voice was weak and sounded far away in his own ears. "My son—does—not—attend the public schools."

Someone in the rear of the room laughed, and the atmosphere lightened at once. Plainly Pavageau was an idiot, and His Honor too far above him; too much of a gentleman to notice him. Grabért con-tinued calmly: The gentleman—there was an unmistakable sneer in this word, habit if nothing else, and not even fear could restrain him—"the gentleman doubtless intended a little pleasantry, but I shall have to fine him for contempt of court."

"As you will," replied Pavageau, and he flashed another look at Grabért. It was a look of insolent triumph and derision. His Honor's eyes dropped beneath it.

"What did that man mean, Father, by saying you should take me out of school?" asked Vannier on his way home.

He was provoked, my son, because he had lost his case, and when a man is provoked, he is likely to say silly things By the way, Vannier, I hope you won't say anything to your mother about the incident. It would only annoy her."

For the public, the incident was forgotten as soon as it had closed, but for Grabért, it was indelibly stamped on his memory; a scene that shrieked in his mind and stood out before him at every footstep he took. Again and again as he tossed on a sleepless bed did he see the cold flash of Pavageau's eyes, and hear his quiet accusation. How did he know? Where had he gotten his information? For he spoke, not as one who makes a random shot in anger; but as one who knows, who has known a long while, and who is betrayed by irritation into playing his trump card too early in the game.

He passed a wretched week, wherein it seemed that his every footstep was dogged, his every gesture watched and recorded. He fancied that Elise, even, was suspecting him When he took his judicial seat each morning, it seemed that every eye in the courtroom was fastened upon him in derision; everyone who spoke, it seemed, were but biding their time to shout the old village street refrain which had haunted him all his life, "Nigger!—Nigger!—White nigger!"

Finally, he could stand it no longer, and with leaden feet and furtive glances to the right and left for fear he might be seen, he went up a flight of dusty stairs in an Exchange Alley building, which led to Pavageau's office.

The latter was frankly surprised to see him. He made a polite attempt to conceal it, however. It was the first time in his legal life that Grabért had ever sought out a Negro; the first time that he had ever voluntarily opened conversation with one.

He mopped his forehead nervously as he took the chair Pavageau offered him; he stared about the room for an instant; then with a sudden, almost brutal directness, he turned on the lawyer.

"See here, what did you mean by that remark you made in court the other day?"

"I meant just what I said," was the cool reply.

Grabért paused, "Why did you say it?" he asked slowly.

"Because I was a fool. I should have kept my mouth shut until another time, should I not?"

"Pavageau," said Grabért softly, "let's not fence. Where did you get your information?"

Pavageau paused for an instant. He put his fingertips together and closed his eyes as one who meditates. Then he said with provoking calmness,

"You seem anxious—well, I don't mind letting you know. It doesn't really matter."

"Yes, yes," broke in Grabért impatiently.

"Did you ever hear of a Madame Guichard of Hospital Street?"

The sweat broke out on the judge's brow as he replied weakly, "Yes."

"Well, I am her nephew."

"And she?"

"Is dead. She told me about you once—with pride, let me say. No one else knows."

Grabért sat dazed. He had forgotten about Madame Guichard She had never entered into his calculations. Pavageau turned to his desk with a sigh as if he wished the interview were ended. Grabért rose.

"If—if—this were known—to—to—my—my wife, he said thickly, "it would hurt her very much.

His head was swimming. He had had to appeal to this man, and to appeal in his wife's name. His wife, whose name he scarcely spoke to men whom he considered his social equals.

Pavageau looked up quickly. It happens that I often have cases in your court," he spoke deliberately. "I am willing, if I lose fairly, to give up; but I do not like to have a decision made against me because my opponent is of a different complexion from mine, or because the decision against me would please a certain class of people. I only ask what I have never had from you—fair play."

"I understand," said Grabért

He admired Pavageau more than ever as he went out of his office, yet this admiration was tempered by the knowledge that this man was the only person in the whole world who possessed positive knowledge of his secret. He groveled in a self-abasement at his position; and yet he could not but feel a certain relief that the vague formless fear which had hitherto dogged his life and haunted it had taken on a definite shape. He knew where it was now; he could lay his hands on it and fight it.

But with what weapons? There were none offered him save a substantial backing down from his position on certain questions; the position that had been his for so long that he was almost known by it. For in the quiet deliberate sentence of Pavageau's, he read that he must cease all the oppression, all the little injustices which he had offered Pavageau's clientele. He must act now as his convictions and secret sympathies and affiliations had bidden him act; not as prudence and fear and cowardice had made him act.

Then what would be the result? he asked himself. Would not the suspicions of the people be aroused by this sudden change in his manner? Would not they begin to question and to wonder? Would not someone remember Pavageau's remark that morning and, putting two and two together start some rumor flying? His heart sickened again at the thought.

There was a banquet that night. It was in his honor, and he was to speak and the thought was distasteful to him beyond measure. He knew how it all would be. He would be hailed with shouts and acclamations, as the finest flower of civilization. He would be listened to deferentially, and younger men would go away holding him in their hearts as a truly worthy model. When all the while—

He threw back his head and laughed. Oh, what a glorious revenge he had on those little white village boys! How he had made a race atone for Wilson's insult in the courtroom; for the man in the restaurant at whom Ward had laughed so uproariously; for all the affronts seen and unseen given these people of his own whom he had denied. He had taken a diploma from their most exclusive college; he had broken down the barriers of their social world; he had taken the highest possible position among them; and aping their own ways, had shown them that he too could despise this inferior race they despised. Nay, he had taken for his wife the best woman among them all, and she had borne him a son. Ha, ha! What a joke on them all!

And he had not forgotten the black and yellow boys either. They had stoned him too, and he had lived to spurn them; to look down upon them, and to crush them at every possible turn from his seat on the bench. Truly, his life had not been wasted.

He had lived forty-nine years now, and the zenith of his power was not yet reached. There was much more to do, much more, and he was going to do it. He owed it to Elise and the boy. For their sake he must go on and on and keep his tongue still, and truckle to Pavageau and suffer alone. Someday, perhaps, he would have a grandson, who would point with pride to "my grandfather, the famous Judge Grabért!" Ah, that in itself was a reward. To have founded a dynasty; to bequeath to others that which he had never possessed himself, and the lack of which had made his life a misery.

It was a banquet with a political significance; one that meant a virtual triumph for Judge Grabért in the next contest for the District Judge. He smiled around at the eager faces which were turned up to his as he arose to speak. The tumult of applause which had greeted his rising had died away, and an expectant hush fell on the room.

"What a sensation I could make now," he thought. He had but to open his mouth and cry out, "Fools! Fools! I whom you are honoring, I am one of the despised ones. Yes, I'm a nigger—do you hear, a nigger!" What a temptation it was to end the whole miserable farce. If he were alone in the world, if it were not for Elise and the boy, he would, just to see their horror and wonder. How they would shrink from him! But what could they do? They could take away his office; but his wealth, and his former successes, and his learning, they could not touch. Well, he must speak and he must remember Elise and the boy.

Every eye was fixed on him in eager expectancy. Judge Grabért's speech was expected to outline the policy of their faction in the coming campaign. He turned to the chairman at the head of the table.

"Mr. Chairman," he began, and paused again. How peculiar it was that in the place of the chairman there sat Grandmere Grabért as she had been wont to sit on the steps of the tumbledown cottage in the village. She was looking at him sternly and bidding him give an account of his life since she had kissed him good-bye ere he had sailed down the river to New Orleans. He was surprised, and not a little annoyed. He had expected to address the chairman, not Grandmere Grabért. He cleared his throat and frowned.

"Mr. Chairman," he said again. Well, what was the use of addressing her that way? She would not understand him. He would call her Grandmere, of course. Were they not alone again on the cottage steps at twilight with the cries of the little brutish boys ringing derisively from the distant village square?

"Grandmere," he said softly, "you don't understand—" and then he was sitting down in his seat pointing one finger angrily at her because the other words would not come. They stuck in his throat, and he choked and beat the air with his hands. When the men crowded around him with water and hastily improvised fans, he fought them away wildly and desperately with furious curses that came from his blackened lips. For were they not all boys with stones to pelt him because he wanted to play with them? He would run away to Grandmere, who would soothe him and comfort him. So he arose and, stumbling, shrieking, and beating them back from him, ran the length of the hall and fell across the threshold of the door.

The secret died with him, for Pavageau's lips were ever sealed.

"As the Lord Lives, He is One of Our Mother's Children"

by
PAULINE E. HOPKINS

IT WAS SATURDAY AFTERNOON in a large Western town, and the Rev. Septimus Stevens sat in his study writing down the headings for his Sunday sermon. It was slow work; somehow the words would not flow with their usual ease, although his brain was teeming with ideas. He had written for his heading at the top of the sheet these words for a text: "As I live, he is one of our mother's children." It was to be a great effort on the Negro question, and the reverend gentleman, with his New England training, was in full sympathy with his subject. He had jotted down a few headings under it, when he came to a full stop, his mind simply refused to work. Finally, with a sigh, he opened the compartment in his desk where his sermons were packed and began turning over those old creations in search of something suitable for the morrow.

Suddenly the whistles in all directions began to blow wildly. The Rev. Septimus hurried to the window, threw it open, and leaned out, anxious to learn the cause of the wild clamor. Could it be another of the terrible "cave-ins that were the terror of every mining district? Men were pouring out of the mines as fast as they could come up. The crowds which surged through the streets night and day were rushing to meet them. Hundreds of policemen were about; each corner was guarded by a squad commanded by a sergeant. The police and the mob were evidently working together. Tramp, tramp, on they rushed; down the serpentine boulevard for nearly two miles they went swelling like an angry torrent. In front of the open window

93

where stood the white-faced clergyman, they paused. A man mounted the empty barrel and harangued the crowd: "I am from Dover City, gentlemen, and I have come here today to assist you in teaching the blacks a lesson. I have killed a nigger before," he yelled, "and in revenge of the wrong wrought upon you and yours, I am willing to kill again. The only way you can teach these niggers a lesson is to go to the jail and lynch these men as an object lesson. String them up! That is the only thing to do. Kill them, string them up, lynch them! I will lead you. On to the prison and lynch Jones and Wilson, the black fiends!" With a hoarse shout, in which were mingled cries like the screams of enraged hyenas and the snarls of tigers, they rushed on.

Nora, the cook, burst open the study door, pale as a sheet, and dropped at the minister's feet. "Mother of God!" she cried. "And is it the end of the world?"

On the maddened men rushed from north, south, east, and west, armed with everything from a brick to a horsepistol. In the melee a man was shot down. Somebody planted a long knife in the body of a little black newsboy for no apparent reason. Every now and then a Negro would be overwhelmed somewhere on the outskirts of the crowd and left beaten to a pulp. Then they reached the jail and battered in the door.

The solitary watcher at the window tried to move, but could not; terror had stricken his very soul, and his white lips moved in articulate prayer. The crowd surged back. In the midst was only one man; for some reason, the other was missing. A rope was knotted about his neck—charged with murder, himself about to be murdered. The hands which drew the rope were too swift, and half-strangled, the victim fell. The crowd halted, lifted him up, loosened the rope and let the wretch breathe.

He was a grand man—physically—black as ebony, tall, straight, deep-chested, every fiber full of that life so soon to be quenched. Lucifer, just about to be cast out of heaven, could not have thrown around a glance of more scornful pride. What might not such a man have been, if—but it was too late. "Run fair, boys," said the prisoner, calmly, "run fair! You keep up your end of the rope, and I'll keep up mine."

The crowd moved a little more slowly, and the minister saw the tall form "keeping up" its end without a tremor of hesitation. As they neared the telegraph pole, with its outstretched arm, the watcher summoned up his lost strength, grasped the curtain, and pulled it down to shut out the dreadful sight. Then came a moment of ominous silence The man of God sank upon his knees to pray for the passing soul. A thousand-voiced cry of brutal triumph arose in cheers for the work that had been done, and curses and imprecations, and they who had hunted a man out of life hurried off to hunt for gold.

To and fro on the white curtain swung the black silhouette of what had been a man.

For months the minister heard in the silence of the night phantom echoes of those frightful voices, and awoke, shuddering, from some dream whose vista was closed by that lack figure swinging in the air.

About a month after this happening, the rector was returning from a miner's cabin in the mountains where a child lay dying. The child haunted him; he thought of his own motherless boy, and a fountain of pity overflowed in his heart. He had dismounted and was walking along the road to the ford at the creek which just here cut the path fairly in two.

The storm of the previous night had refreshed all nature and had brought out the rugged beauty of the landscape in all its grandeur. The sun had withdrawn his last dazzling rays from the eastern highlands upon which the lone traveler gazed, and now they were fast veiling themselves in purple night shadows that rendered them momentarily more grand and mysterious. The man of God stood a moment with uncovered head repeating aloud some lines from a great Russian poet:

"O Thou eternal One! whose presence bright
All space doth occupy, all motion guide;
Unchanged through time's all devastating flight;
Thou only God! There is no God beside
Being above all beings, Mighty One!
Whom none can comprehend and none explore."

Another moment passed in silent reverence of the All-Wonderful, before he turned to remount his horse and enter the waters of the creek. The creek was very much swollen, and he found it hard to keep the ford. Just as he was midway the stream, he saw something lying half in the water on the other bank. Approaching nearer, he discovered it to be a man, apparently unconscious. Again dismounting, he tied his horse to a sapling and went up to the inert figure, ready, like the Samaritan of old, to succor the wayside fallen. The man opened his deep-set eyes and looked at him keenly. He was gaunt, haggard, and despairing, and soaking wet.

"Well, my man, what is the matter?" Rev. Mr. Stevens had a very direct way of going at things.

"Nothing," was the sullen response.

"Can't I help you? You seem ill. Why are you lying in the water?"

"I must have fainted and fallen in the creek," replied the man, answering the last question first. "I've tramped from Colorado hunting for work. I'm penniless, have no home, haven't had much to eat for a week, and now I've got a touch of your damn mountain fever." He shivered as if with a chill and smiled faintly.

The man, from his speech, was well educated and, in spite of his pitiful situation, had an air of good breeding barring his profanity.

"What's your name?" asked Stevens, glancing him over sharply as he knelt beside the man and deftly felt his pulse and laid a cool hand on the fevered brow.

"Stone—George Stone."

Stevens got up. "Well, Stone, try to get on my horse, and I'll take you to the rectory. My housekeeper and I together will manage to make you more comfortable."

So it happened that George Stone became a guest at the parsonage and, later, sexton of the church. In that gold mining region, where new people came and went constantly and new excitements were things of everyday occurrence, and new faces as plenty as old ones, nobody asked or cared where the new sexton came from. He did his work quietly and thoroughly and quite won Nora's heart by his handy ways about the house. He had a room under the eaves and seemed thankful and content. Little Flip, the rector's son took a special liking to him, and he, on his side, worshipped the golden-haired child and was never tired of playing with him and inventing things for his amusement.

The reverend sets a heap by the boy," he said to Nora one day in reply to her accusation that he spoiled the boy and there was no living with him since Stone's advent. "He won't let me thank him for what he's done for me, but he can't keep me from loving the child."

One day in September, while passing along the street Rev. Stevens had his attention called to a flaming poster on the side of a fence by the remarks of a crowd of men near him. He turned and read it:

$1,500 REWARD!
The above reward will be paid for information leading to the arrest of "Gentleman Jim," charged with complicity m the murder of Jerry Mason.

This nigger is six feet, three inches tall, weight one hundred and sixty pounds. He escaped from jail when his pal was lynched two months ago by a citizen's committee. It is thought that he is in the mountains, etc. He is well educated, and might be taken for a white man. Wore, when last seen, blue jumper and overalls and cowhide boots.

He read it the second time, and he was dimly conscious of seeing, like a vision in the brain, a man playing about the parsonage with little Flip.

"I knowed him. I worked a spell with him over in Lone Tree Gulch before he got down on his luck," spoke a man at his side who was reading the poster with him. Jones and him was two of the smartest and peaceful niggers I ever seed. But Jerry Mason kinder sat on 'em both; never could tell why, only some white men can't 'bide a nigger any more than a dog can a cat; it's a natural antipathy. I'm free to say the niggers seemed harmless, but you can't tell what a man'll do when his blood's up."

He turned to the speaker. "What will happen if they catch him?"

"Lynch him sure; there's been a lot of trouble over there lately. I wouldn't give a toss-up for him if they get their hands on him once more."

Rev. Stevens pushed his way through the crowd and went slowly down the street to the church. He found Stone there sweeping and dusting. Saying that he wanted to speak with him, he led the way to the study. Facing around upon him suddenly, Stevens said, gravely: "I want you to tell me the truth. Is your real name Stone, and are you a Negro.

A shudder passed over Stone's strong frame, then he answered, while his eyes never left the troubled face before him, "I am a Negro, and my name is not Stone.

"You said that you had tramped from Colorado.

"I hadn't. I was hiding in the woods; I had been there a month ago. I lied to you."

"Is it all a lie?"

Stone hesitated, and then said: "I was meaning to tell you the first night, but somehow I couldn't. I was afraid you'd turn me out; and I was sick and miserable—

"Tell me the truth now."

"I will; I'll tell you the God's truth."

He leaned his hand on the back of a chair to steady himself; he was trembling violently. "I came out West from Wilmington, North

Carolina, Jones and I together. We were both college men and chums from childhood. All our savings were in the business we had at home, when the leading men of the town conceived the idea of driving the Negroes out, and the Wilmington tragedy began. Jones was unmarried, but I lost wife and children that night—burned to death when the mob fired our home. When we got out here, we took up claims in the mountains. They were a rough crowd after we struck pay dirt, but Jones and I kept to ourselves and got along all right until Mason joined the crowd. He was from Wilmington; knew us, and took delight in tormenting us. He was a fighting man, but we wouldn't let him push us into trouble."

"You didn't quarrel with him, then?"

The minister gazed at Stone keenly. He seemed a man to trust. "Yes, I did. We didn't want trouble, but we couldn't let Mason rob us. We three had hot words before a big crowd; that was all there was to it that night. In the morning, Mason lay dead upon our claim. He'd been shot by someone. My partner and I were arrested, brought to this city, and lodged in the jail over there. Jones was lynched! God, can I ever forget that hooting, yelling crowd, and the terrible fight to get away! Somehow I did it—you know the rest."

"Stone, there's a reward for you, and a description of you as you were the night I found you."

Gentleman Jim's face was ashy. "I'll never be taken alive. They'll kill me for what I never did!"

"Not unless I speak. I am in sore doubt what course to take; If I give you up, the vigilantes will hang you."

"I'm a lost man," said the Negro helplessly, "but I'll never be taken alive."

Stevens walked up and down the room once or twice. It was a human life in his hands. If left to the law to decide, even then in this particular case the Negro stood no chance. It was an awful question to decide. One more turn up and down the little room and suddenly stopping, he flung himself upon his knees in the middle of the room and, raising his clasped hands, cried aloud for heavenly guidance. Such a prayer as followed, the startled listener had never before heard anywhere. There was nothing of rhetorical phrases, nothing of careful thought in the construction of sentences; it was the outpouring of a pure soul asking for help from its Heavenly Father with all the trustfulness of a little child. It came in a torrent, a flood; it wrestled mightily for the blessing it sought. Rising to his feet when his prayer was finished, Rev. Stevens said, "Stone,—you are to remain

Stone, you know—it is best to leave things as they are. Go back to work."

The man raised his bowed head.

"You mean you're not going to give me up?"

"Stay here till the danger is past; then leave for other parts."

Stone's face turned red, then pale; his voice trembled, and tears were in the gray eyes. "I can't thank you, Mr. Stevens, but if ever I get the chance you'll find me grateful."

"Al right, Stone, all right," and the minister went back to his writing.

That fall the Rev. Septimus Stevens went to visit his old New England home—he and Flip. He was returning home the day before Thanksgiving, with his widowed mother, who had elected to leave old associations and take charge of her son's home. It was a dim-colored day.

Engineers were laying out a new road near a place of swamps and oozy ground and dead, wet grass, overarched by leafless, desolate boughs. They were eating their lunch now, seated about on the trunks of fallen trees. The jokes were few, scarcely a pun seasoned the meal. The day was a dampener; that the morrow was a holiday did not kindle merriment.

Stone sat a little apart from the rest. He had left Rev. Stevens when he got this job in another state. They had voted him moody and unsociable long ago—a man who broods forever upon his wrongs is not a comfortable companion; he never gave any one a key to his moods. He shut himself up in his haunted room—haunted by memory—and no one interfered with him.

The afternoon brought a change in the weather. There was a strange hush, as if Nature were holding her breath. But it was as a wild beast holds its breath before a spring Suddenly a little chattering wind ran along the ground. It was too weak to lift the sodden leaves, yet it made itself heard in some way and grew stronger. It seemed dizzy and ran about in a circle. There was a pale light over all, a brassy, yellow light, that gave all things a wild look. The chief of the party took an observation and said: "We'd better get home."

Stone lingered. He was paler, older.

The wind had grown vigorous now and began to tear angrily at the trees, twisting the saplings about with invisible hands. There was a rush and a roar that seemed to spread about in every direction. A tree was furiously uprooted and fell directly in front of him; Stone noticed the storm for the first time.

He looked about him in a dazed way and muttered, He s coming on this train, he and the kid!"

The brassy light deepened into darkness. Stone went upon the railroad track and stumbled over something that lay directly over it. It was a huge tree that the wind had lifted in its great strength and whirled over there like thistledown. He raised himself slowly, a little confused by the fall. He took hold of the tree mechanically, but the huge bulk would not yield an inch.

He looked about in the gathering darkness; it was five miles to the station where he might get help. His companions were too far on their way to recall, and there lay a huge mass, directly in the way of the coming train. He had no watch, but he knew it must be nearly six. Soon—very soon—upon the iron pathway, a great train, freighted with life, would dash around the curve to wreck and ruing Again he muttered, "Coming on this train, he and the kid!" He pictured the faces of his benefactor and the little child, so like his own lost one, cold in death; the life crushed out by the cruel wheels. What was it that seemed to strike across the storm and all its whirl of sound—a child's laugh? Nay, something fainter still—the memory of a child's laugh. It was like a breath of spring flowers in the desolate winter— a touch of heart music amid the revel of the storm. A vision of other fathers with children climbing upon their knees, a soft babble of baby voices assailed him.

"God help me to save them!" he cried.

Again and again he tugged at the tree. It would not move. Then he hastened and got an iron bar from among the tools. Again he strove—once—twice—thrice. With a groan the nearest end gave way. Eureka! If only his strength would hold out. He felt it ebbing slowly from him, something seemed to clutch at his heart; his head swam. Again and yet again he exerted all his strength. There came a pro-longed shriek that awoke the echoes. The train was coming. The tree was moving! It was almost off the other rail. The leafless trees seemed to enfold him—to hold him with skeleton arms. "Oh, God save them!" he gasped. "Our times are in Thy hand!"

Something struck him a terrible blow. The agony was ended. Stone was dead.

Rev. Stevens closed his eyes, with a deadly faintness creeping over him, when he saw how near the trainload of people had been to destruction. Only God had saved them at the eleventh hour through the heroism of Stone, who lay dead upon the track, the life crushed out of him by the engine. An inarticulate thanksgiving rose to his lips as soft and clear came the sound of distant church bells, calling to weekly prayer, like "horns of Elfland softly blowing."

Sunday, a week later, Rev. Septimus Stevens preached the greatest sermon of his life. They had found the true murderer of Jerry Mason, and Jones and Gentleman Jim were publicly exonerated by a repentant community.

On this Sunday Rev. Stevens preached the funeral sermon of Gentleman Jim. The church was packed to suffocation by a motley assemblage of men in all stages of dress and undress, but there was a sincerity in their hearts as they listened to the preacher's burning words: "As the Lord lives, he is one of our mother's children."

My House and a Glimpse of My Life Therein

by
<u>JESSIE REDMOND FAUSET</u>

FAR AWAY ON THE TOP of a gently sloping hill stands my house. On one side the hill slopes down into a valley, the site of a large country town; on the other it descends into a forest, thick with lofty trees and gréen, growing things. Here in stately solitude amid such surroundings towers my dwelling; its dull-red brick is barely visible through the thick ivy, but the gleaming tops of its irregular roof and sloping gables catch the day's sunlight and crown it with a crown of gold.

An irregular, rambling building is this house of mine, built on no particular plan, following no order save that of desire and fancy. Peculiarly jutting rooms appear, and unsuspected towers and bay-windows,—the house seems almost to have built itself and to have followed its own will in so doing. If there be any one distinct feature at all, it is that halls long and very broad traverse the various parts of the house, separating a special set of rooms here, making another division there. Splendid halls are these, with fireplaces and cozy arm-chairs, and delightful, dark corners, and mysterious closets, and broad stairs. Just the place in winter for a host of young people to gather before the fireplace and, with popcorn and chestnuts, stories and apples, laugh away the speeding hours, while the wind howls without.

The hall on the ground floor has smaller corridors that branch off and lead at their extremity into the garden. Surely, no parterre of the East, perfumed with all the odors of Araby, and peopled with houris, was ever so fair as my garden! Surely, nowhere does the snow lie so pure and smooth and deep, nowhere are the evergreen trees so very tall and stately as in my garden in winter! Most glorious is it in late spring and early June. Out on the green, green sward I sit under the blossoming trees; in sheer delightful idleness I spend my hours, listening to the blending of wind-song with the sweet singing of little birds. If a shower threatens, I flee across my garden's vast expanse, past the gorgeous rosebushes and purple lilacs, and safe within my little summer-house, watch the "straight-falling rain," and think of other days, and sighing, wish that Kathleen and I had not parted in anger that far-off morning.

When the shower ceases, I hasten down the broad path, under the shelter of lofty trees, until I reach one of my house's many doors. Once within, but still in idle mood, I perch myself on a window-seat and look toward the town. Tall spires and godly church steeples rise before me; high above all climbs the town clock; farther over in the west, smoke is curling from the foundries. How busy is the life beyond my house! Through the length of the long hall to the window at the opposite side I go and watch the friendly nodding of tall trees and the tender intercourse of all this beautiful green life. Suddenly the place becomes transformed—this is an enchanted forest, the Forest Morgraunt —in and out among the trees pass valiant knights and distressed ladies. Prosper le Gai rides to the rescue of Isoult la Desirous. Surely, the forest life beyond my house is full of purpose and animation, too.

From the window I roam past the sweet, familiar chambers, to the attic staircase, with its half-hidden angles and crazy old baluster. Up to the top of the house I go, to a dark little store-room under the eaves. I open the trap-door in the middle of the ceiling, haul down a small ladder, mount its deliciously wobbly length, and behold, I am in my chosen domain—a queen come into her very own! If I choose I can convert it into a dread and inaccessible fortress, by drawing up my ladder and showering nutshells and acorns down on the heads of would-be intruders. Safe from all possible invasion, I browse through the store of old, old magazines and quaint books and journals, or wander half-timidly through my infinite unexplored land of mystery, picking my way past heaps of delightful rubbish and strong, secret chests, fancying goblins in the shadowy corners, or watching from the little windows the sunbeams play on the garden, and the gray-blue mist hanging far off over the hollow valley.

From such sights and fancies I descend to my library, there to supplement my flitting ideas with the fixed conception of others.

Although I love every brick and little bit of mortar in my dwelling, my library is of all portions the very dearest to me. In this part of the house, more than anyplace else, have those irregular rooms been added, to receive my ever-increasing store of books. In the large room, —the library proper,—is a broad, old-fashioned fireplace, and on the rug in front I lie and read, and read again, all the dear simple tales of earlier days, *Mother Goose, Alice in Wonderland, The Arabian Nights;* here, too, I revel in modern stories of impossible adventure. But when a storm rises at night, say, and the rain beats and dashes, and all without is raging, I draw a huge, red armchair before the fire and curl into its hospitable depths.

> *And there I sit*
> *Reading old things,*
> *Of knights and damsels,*
> *While the wind sings—*
> *Oh, drearily sings!*

Off in one of the little side-rooms stands my desk, covered with books that have caught my special fancy and awakened my thoughts. This is my *living*-room, where I spend my moods of bitterness and misunderstanding, and questioning, and joy, too, I think. Often in the midst of a heap of books, the Rubaiyat and a Bible, Walter Pater's essays, and *Robert Elsmere* and *Aurora Leigh,* and books of belief, of insinuation, of open unbelief, I bow my head on my desk in a passion of doubt and ignorance and longing, and ponder, ponder. Here on this desk is a book in which I jot down all the little, beautiful word-wonders, whose meanings are so often unknown to me, but whose very mystery I love. I write, "In Vishnu Land what Avatar?" and "After the red pottage comes the exceedingly bitter cry," and all the other sweet, incomprehensible fragments that haunt my memory so.

High up on many of the shelves in the many rooms are books as yet unread by me, Schopenhauer and Gorky, Petrarch and Sappho, Goethe and Kant and Schelling; much of Ibsen, Plato and Ennius and Firdausi, and Lafcadio Hearn,—a few of these in the original. With such reading in store for me, is not my future rich?

Can such a house as this one of mine be without immediate and vivid impression on its possessor? First and most of all, it imbues me with a strong sense of home; banishment from my house would surely be life's most bitter sorrow. It is so eminently and fixedly mine, my very own, that the mere possession of it,—a house not yours or another's, but mine, to live in as I will,—is very sweet to me. It is absolutely my soul's desire. With this sense of ownership, a sense which is deeper than I can express, a sense which is almost a longing for some unknown, unexplainable, entire possession—passionate, spiritual absorption of my dwelling—comes a feeling that is almost terror. Is it right to feel thus, to have this vivid, permeating, and yet wholly intellectual enjoyment of the material loveliness and attractiveness of my house? May this not be perhaps a sensuality of the mind, whose influence may be more insidious, more pernicious, more powerful to unfit me or t e real duties of life than are other lower and yet more open forms of enjoyment? Oh, I pray not! My house is inexpressibly dear to me, but the light of the ideal beyond, "the light that never was on sea or land," is dearer still.

This, then, is my house, and this, in measure, is my life in my house. Here amid my favourite books, and pictures, and fancies, and longings, and sweet mysteries, shall old age come upon me, in fashion most inglorious, but in equal degree most peaceful and happy. *Perhaps*—that is! For after all my house is constructed of dream-fabric, and the place of its building is—*Spain!*

The Typewriter

by
DOROTHY WEST

IT OCCURRED TO HIM, as he eased past the bulging knees of an Irish wash lady and forced an apologetic passage down the aisle of the crowded car, that more than anything m all the world he wanted not to go home. He began to wish passionately that he had never been born that he had never been married, that he had never been the means of life's coming into the world. He knew quite suddenly that he hated his flat and his family and his friends. n most of all the Incessant thing that would "clatter clatter until every nerve screamed aloud, and the words of the evening paper danced crazily before him, and the insane desire to crush and kill set his fingers twitching

He shuffled down the street, an abject little man of fifty-odd years, in an ageless overcoat that flapped in the wind He was cold, and he hated the North, and particularly Boston, and saw suddenly a barefoot pickaninny sitting on a fence in the hot Southern sun with a piece of steaming corn bread and a piece of fried salt pork in either grimy hand.

He was tired, and he wanted his supper, but he didn't want the beans, and frankfurters, and light bread that Net would undoubtedly have. That Net had had every Monday night since that regrettable moment fifteen years before when he had told her—innocently—that such a supper tasted "right nice. Kinda change from what we always has."

He mounted the four brick steps leading to his door and pulled at the bell; but there was no answering ring. It was broken again, and in a mental flash he saw himself with a multitude of tools and a box of matches shivering in the vestibule after supper. He began to pound lustily on the door and wondered vaguely if his hand would bleed if

106

he smashed the glass. He hated the sight of blood. It sickened him.

Some one was running down the stairs. Daisy probably. Millie would be at that infernal thing, pounding, pounding.

. . . He entered. The chill of the house swept him. His child was wrapped in a coat. She whispered solemnly, "Poppa, Miz Hicks an' Miz Berry's awful mad. They going to move if they can't get more heat. The furnace's been out all day. Mama couldn't fix it." He said hurriedly, "I'll go right down. I'll go right down." He hoped Mrs. Hicks wouldn't pull open her door and glare at him. She was large and domineering, and her husband was a bully. If her husband ever struck him, it would kill him. He hated life, but he didn't want to die. He was afraid of God and in his wildest flights of fancy couldn't imagine himself an angel. He went softly down the stairs.

He began to shake the furnace fiercely. And he shook into it every wrong, mumbling softly under his breath. He began to think back over his uneventful years, and it came to him as rather a shock that he had never sworn in all his life. He wondered uneasily if he dared say "damn." It was taken for granted that a man swore when he tended a stubborn furnace. And his strongest interjection was "Great balls of fire!"

The cellar began to warm, and he took off his inadequate overcoat that was streaked with dirt. Well, Net would have to clean that. He'd be damned—! It frightened him and thrilled him He wanted suddenly to rush upstairs and tell Mrs. Hicks if she didn't like the way he was running things she could get out. But he heaped another shovelful of coal on the fire and sighed. He would never be able to get away from himself and the routine of years.

He thought of that eager Negro lad of seventeen who had come North to seek his fortune. He had walked jauntily down Boylston Street, and even his own kind had laughed at the incongruity of him. But he had thrown up his head and promised himself: "You'll have an office here someday. With plate-glass windows and a real mahogany desk." But, though he didn't know it then, he was not the progressive type. And he became successively, in the years bellboy, porter, waiter, cook, and finally janitor in a downtown office building.

He had married Net when he was thirty-three and a waiter. He had married her partly because—though he might not have admitted it—there was no one to eat the expensive delicacies the generous cook gave him every night to bring home. And partly because he dared hope there might be a son to fulfill his dreams. But Millie had come, and after her twin girls who had died within two weeks, then Daisy, and it was tacitly understood that Net was done with child-bearing.

Life, though flowing monotonously, had flowed peacefully enough until that sucker of sanity became a sitting room fixture. Intuitively at the very first he had felt its undesirability. He had suggested hesitatingly that they couldn't afford it. Three dollars the eighth of every month. Three dollars: food and fuel. Times were hard, and the twenty dollars apiece the respective husbands of Miz Hicks and Miz Berry irregularly paid was only five dollars more than the thirty-five a month he paid his own Hebraic landlord. And the Lord knew his salary was little enough. At which point Net spoke her piece, her voice rising shrill o knows I never complain 'bout nothin'. Ain't no other woman got less than me. I been wearin' this same dress here five years, an' I'll wear it another five. But I don't want nothin'. I ain't never wanted nothin'. An' when I does as, it's only for my children. You're a poor sort of father if you can't give that child jes' three dollars a month to rent that typewriter. Ain't another girl in school ain't got one. An most of 'ems bought an' paid for. You know yourself how Millie is. She wouldn't as' me for it till she had to. An I ain't going to disappoint her. She's goin' to get that typewriter Saturday, mark my words."

On a Monday then it had been installed. And in the months that followed, night after night he listened to the murderous "tack, tack, tack" that was like a vampire slowly drinking his blood. If only he could escape. Bar a door against the sound of it. But tied hand and foot by the economic fact that "Lord knows we can't afford to have fires burnin' an' lights lit all over the flat. You all gotta set in one room. An' when you get tired settin' you can go to bed. Gas bill was sump'n scandalous last' month."

He heaped a final shovelful of coal on the fire and watched the first blue flames. Then, his overcoat under his arm, he mounted the cellar stairs. Mrs. Hicks was standing in her kitchen door, arms akimbo. "It's warmin'," she volunteered.

"Yeah"—he was conscious of his grime-streaked face and hands—"it's warmin'. I'm sorry 'bout all day."

She folded her arms across her ample bosom. Tending a furnace ain't a woman's work. I don't blame your wife none 'tall."

Unsuspecting he was grateful. "Yeah, it's pretty hard for a woman. I always look after it 'fore I goes to work, but some days it jes' ac's up."

"Y'oughta have a janitor, that's what y'ought," she flung at him. "The same colored man that tends them apartments would be willin'. Mr. Taylor has him. It takes a man to run a furnace, and when the man's away all day—

"I know," he interrupted, embarrassed and hurt, I know. Tha's right, Miz Hicks, tha's right. But I ain't in a position to make no improvements. Times is hard."

She surveyed him critically. "Your wife called down 'bout three times while you was in the cellar. I reckon she wants you for supper."

"Thanks," he mumbled, and escaped up the back stairs

He hung up his overcoat in the closet, telling himself, a little lamely, that it wouldn't take him more'n a minute to clean it up himself after supper. After all Net was tired and probably worried what with Miz Hicks and all. And he hated men who made slaves of their womenfolk. Good old Net.

He tidied up in the bathroom, washing his face and hands carefully and cleanly so as to leave no—or very little —stain on the roller towel. It was hard enough for Net, God knew.

He entered the kitchen. The last spirals of steam were rising from his supper. One thing about Net, she served a full plate. He smiled appreciatively at her unresponsive back bent over the kitchen sink. There was no one could bake beans just like Net's. And no one who could find a market with frankfurters quite so fat.

He sank down at his place. "Evenin', hon."

He saw her back stiffen. "If your supper's cold, 'tain't my fault. I called and called."

He said hastily, "It's fine, Net, fine. Piping."

She was the usual tired housewife. "Y'oughta ate your supper 'fore you fooled with that furnace. I ain't bothered bout them niggers. I got all my dishes washed 'cept yours. An' I hate to mess up my kitchen after I once get it straightened up."

He was humble. "I'll give that old furnace an extra looking after in the mornin'. It'll last all day tomorrow, hon."

"An' on top of that," she continued, unheeding him and giving a final wrench to her dish towel, "that confounded bell don't ring. An'—"

"I'll fix it after supper," he interposed hastily

She hung up her dish towel and came to stand before him looming large and yellow. "An' that old Miz Berry, she claim she was expectin' company. An' she knows they must a come an gone while she was in her kitchen an' couldn't be at her winder to watch for 'em.

109

Old liar," she brushed back a lock of naturally straight hair. "She was-n't expecting nobody."

"Well, you know how some folks are—"

"Fools! Half the world," was her vehement answer. "I'm goin' in the front room an' set down a spell. I've been on my feet all day. Leave them dishes on the table. God knows I'm tired, but I'll come back an' wash 'em." But they both knew, of course, that he, very clumsily, would.

At precisely quarter past nine when he, strained at last to the breaking point, uttering an inhuman, strangled cry, flung down his paper, clutched at his throat, and sprang to his feet, Millie's surprised young voice, shocking: him to normalcy, heralded the first of that series of great moments that every humble little middle-class man eventually experiences.

"What's the matter, Poppa? You sick? I wanted you to help me."

He drew out his handkerchief and wiped his hot hands. "I declare I must 'a' fallen asleep an' had a nightmare. No, I ain't sick. What you want, hon?"

"Dictate me a letter, Poppa. I can do sixty words a minute.—You know, like a business letter. You know, like those men in your building dictate to their stenographers. Don't you hear 'em sometimes?"

"Oh, sure, I know, hon. Poppa'll help you. Sure. I hear that Mr. Browning—sure."

Net rose. "Guess I'll put this child to bed. Come on now, Daisy, without no fuss.—Then I'll run up to Pa's. He ain't been well all week."

When the door closed behind them, he crossed to his daughter, conjured the image of Mr. Browning in the process of dictating, so arranged himself, and coughed importantly.

"Well, Millie—"

"Oh, Poppa, is that what you'd call your stenographer? she teased. "And anyway pretend I'm really one—and you're really my boss, and this letter's real important."

A light crept into his dull eyes. Vigor through his thin blood. In a brief moment the weight of years fell from him like a cloak. Tired, bent, little old man that he was, he smiled, straightened, tapped impressively against his teeth with a toil-stained finger, and became that enviable emblem of American life: a business man.

"You be Miz Hicks, huh, honey? 'Course we can't both use the same name. I'll be J. Lucius Jones. J. Lucius. All them real big doin' men use their middle names. Jus' kinda looks big doin, doncha think,

110

hon? Looks like money, u . J. Lucius. He uttered a sound that was like the proud cluck of a strutting hen. "J. Lucius." It rolled like oil from his tongue.

His daughter twisted impatiently. "Now, Poppa—I mean Mr. Jones, sir—please begin. I am ready for dictation, sir."

He was in that office on Boylston Street, looking through its plate-glass windows, tapping with impatient fingers on its real mahogany desk.

"Ah—Beaker Brothers, Park Square Building, Boston, Mass. Ah—Gentlemen: In reply to yours of the seventh instant would state—"

Every night thereafter in the weeks that followed with Daisy packed off to bed, and Net "gone up to Pa s" or nodding unobtrusively in her corner, there was the chameleon change of a Court Street janitor to J. Lucius Jones, dealer in stocks and bonds. He would stand, posturing, importantly flicking imaginary dust from his coat lapel, or, his hands locked behind his back, he would stride up and own, earnestly and seriously debating the advisability of buying copper with the market in such a fluctuating state Once a week, too. he stopped in at Jerry's and, after a preliminary purchase of cheap cigars, bought the latest trade papers, mumbling an embarrassed explanation "I got a little money. Think I'll invest it in reliable stock.';

The letters Millie typed and subsequently discarded, he rummaged for later, and under cover of writing to his brother in the South, laboriously, with a great many fancy flourishes, signed each neatly typed sheet with the exalted J. Lucius Jones.

Later, when he mustered the courage, he suggested tentatively to Millie that it might be fun—just fun, of course! —to answer his letters. One night—he laughed a good deal louder and longer than necessary—he'd be J. Lucius Jones, and the next night—here he swallowed hard and looked a little frightened—Rockefeller or Vanderbilt or Morgan— just for fun, y'understand! To which Millie gave consent It mattered little to her one way or the other. It was practice, and that was what she needed. Very soon now she'd be in the hundred class. Then maybe she could get a job!

He was growing very careful of his English. Occasionally —and it must be admitted, ashamedly—he made surreptitious ventures into the dictionary. He had to, of course. J. Lucius Jones would never say "Y'got to" when he meant "It is expedient." And, old brain though he was, he learned quickly and easily, juggling words with amazing facility.

Eventually he bought stamps and envelopes—long, important-looking envelopes—and stammered apologetically to Millie, "Honey, Poppa thought it'd help you if you learned to type envelopes, too. Reckon you'll have to do that, too, when you get a job. Poor old man"—he swallowed painfully— "came round selling these envelopes. You know how 'tis. So I had to buy 'em." Which was satisfactory to Millie. If she saw through her father, she gave no sign. After all, it was practice, and Mr. Hennessey had promised the smartest girl in the class a position in the very near future. And she, of course, was smart as a steel trap. Even Mr. Hennessey had said that—though not in just those words.

He had got in the habit of carrying those self-addressed envelopes in his inner pocket where they bulged impressively. And occasionally he would take them out—on the car usually—and smile upon them. This one might be from J. P. Morgan. This one from Henry Ford. And a million dollar deal involved in each. That narrow, little spinster, who, upon his sitting down, had drawn herself away from his contact, was shunning J. Lucius Jones!

Once, led by some sudden, strange impulse, as an outgoing car rumbled up out of the subway, he got out a letter, darted a quick, shamed glance about him, dropped it in an adjacent box, and swung aboard the car, feeling, dazedly, as s he had committed a crime. And the next night he sat in the sitting-room quite on edge until Net said suddenly Look here, a real important letter come today for you, Pa Here 'tis. What you s'pose it says," and he reached out a hand that trembled. He made brief explanation. "Advertisement, hon. Thassal."

They came quite frequently after that, and despite the fact that he knew them by heart, he read them slowly and carefully, rustling the sheet and making inaudible, intelligent comments. He was, in these moments, pathetically earnest.

Monday, as he went about his janitor's duties, he composed in his mind the final letter from J. P. Morgan that would consummate a big business deal. For days now letters had passed between them. J. P. had been at first quite frankly uninterested. He had written tersely and briefly Which was meat to J. Lucius. The compositions of his brain were really the work of an artist. He wrote glowingly of the advantages of a pact between them. Daringly he argued in terms of billions. And at last J. P. had written his next letter would be decisive. Which next letter, this Monday, as he trailed about the office building, was writing itself on his brain.

That night Millie opened the door for him. Her plain face was transformed. "Poppa—Poppa, I got a job! Twelve dollars a week to start with! Isn't that swell!"

He was genuinely pleased. "Honey, I'm glad. Right glad, and went up the stairs, unsuspecting.

He ate his supper hastily, went down into the cellar to see about his fire, returned, and carefully tidied up, informing his reflection in the bathroom mirror, "Well, J. Lucius, you c an expect that final letter any day now."

He entered the sitting-room. The phonograph was playing. Daisy was singing lustily. Strange. Net was talking animatedly to—Millie, busy with needle and thread over a neat little frock. His wild glance darted to the table. The pretty little centerpiece, the bowl and wax flowers all neatly arranged: the typewriter gone from its accustomed place. It seemed an hour before he could speak. He felt himself trembling. Went hot and cold.

"Millie—your typewriter's—gone!"

She made a deft little in-and-out movement with her needle. "It's the eighth, you know. When the man came today for the money, I sent it back. I won't need it no more —now!—The money's on the mantelpiece, Poppa.

"Yeah," he muttered. "All right."

He sank down in his chair, fumbled for the paper, found it.

Net said, "Your poppa wants to read. Stop your noise, Daisy."

She obediently stopped both her noise and the phonograph, took up her book, and became absorbed. Millie went on with her sewing in placid anticipation of the morrow. Net immediately began to nod, gave a curious snort, slept.

Silence. That crowded in on him, engulfed him. That blurred his vision, dulled his brain. Vast, white, impenetrable . . . His ears strained for the old, familiar sound. And silence beat upon them . . . The words of the evening paper jumbled together. He read: J. P. Morgan goes—

It burst upon him. Blinded him. His hands groped for the bulge beneath his coat. Why this—this was the end! The end of those great moments—the end of everything! Bewildering pain tore through him. He clutched at his heart and felt, almost, the jagged edges drive into his hand. A lethargy swept down upon him. He could not move, nor utter sound. He could not pray, nor curse.

Against the wall of that silence J. Lucius Jones crashed and died.

Wedding Day

by
GWENDOLYN BENNETT

HIS NAME WAS PAUL WATSON, and as he shambled down rue Pigalle, he might have been any other Negro of enormous height and size. But as I have said, his name was au Watson. Passing him on the street, you might not have known or cared who he was, but any one of the residents about the great Montmartre district of Paris could have told you who he was as well as many interesting bits of his personal history.

He had come to Paris in the days before colored jazz bands were the style. Back home he had been a prizefighter. In the days when Joe Gans was in his glory, Paul was following the ring, too. He didn't have that fine way about him that Gans had, and for that reason luck seemed to go against him. When he was in the ring, he was like a mad bull, especially if his opponent was a white man. In those days there wasn't any sympathy or nicety about the ring, and so pretty soon all the ringmasters got down on Paul, and he found it pretty hard to get a bout with anyone. Then it was that he worked his way across the Atlantic Ocean on a big liner—in the days before colored jazz bands were the style in Paris.

Things flowed along smoothly for the first few years with Paul's working here and there in the unfrequented places of Paris. On the side he used to give boxing lessons to aspiring youths or gymnastic young women. At that time he was working so steadily that he had little chance to find out what was going on around Paris. Pretty soon, however, he grew to be known among the trainers, and managers began to fix up bouts for him. After one or two successful bouts a little fame began to come into being for him. So it was that after one of the prize-fights, a colored fellow came to his dressing room to con-

114

gratulate him on his success as well as invite him to go to Montmartre to meet "the boys."

Paul had a way about him and seemed to get on with the colored fellows who lived in Montmartre, and when the first Negro jazz band played in a tiny Parisian cafe, Paul was among them playing the banjo. Those first years were without event so far as Paul was concerned. The members of that first band often say now that they wonder how it was that nothing happened during those first seven years, for it was generally known how great was Paul's hatred for American white people. I suppose the tranquillity in the light of what happened afterward was due to the fact that the cafe in which they worked was one in which mostly French people drank and danced, and then too, that was before there were so many Americans visiting Paris. However, everyone had heard Paul speak of his intense hatred of American white folks. It only took two Benedictines to make him start talking about what he would do to the first "Yank" that called him "nigger." But the seven years came to an end, and Paul Watson went to work in a larger cafe with a larger band, patronized almost solely by Americans. I've heard almost every Negro in Montmartre tell about the night that a drunken Kentuckian came into the cafe where Paul was playing and said:

"Look here, Brother, what you all doin' over here?"

"None ya bizness. And looka here, I ain't your brother, see?"

"Jack, do you hear that nigger talkin' like that to me?"

As he said this, he turned to speak to his companion. I have often wished that I had been there to have seen the thing happen myself. Every tale I have heard about it was different, and yet there was something of truth in each of them. Perhaps the nearest one can come to the truth is by saying that Paul beat up about four full-sized white men that night besides doing a great deal of damage to the furniture about the cafe. I couldn't tell you just what did happen. Some of the fellows say that Paul seized the nearest table and mowed down men right and left, others say he took a bottle, then again the story runs that a chair was the instrument of his fury. At any rate, that started Paul Watson on his war against the American white person who brings his native prejudices into the life of Paris.

It is a verity that Paul was the "black terror." The last syllable of the word nigger never passed the lips of a white man without the quick reflex action of Paul's arm and fist to the speaker's jaw. He paid for more glassware and cafe furnishings in the course of the next few years than is easily Imaginable. And yet, there was something likable

115

about Paul. Perhaps that's the reason that he stood in so well with the policemen of the neighborhood. Always some divine power seemed to intervene in his behalf, and he was excused after the payment of a small fine with advice about his future conduct. Finally, there came the night when in a frenzy he shot the two American sailors.

They had not died from the wounds he had given them, hence his sentence had not been one of death but rather a long term of imprisonment. It was a pitiable sight to see Paul sitting in the corner of his cell with his great body hunched almost double. He seldom talked, and when he did, his words were interspersed with oaths about the lowness of "crackers." Then the World War came.

It seems strange that anything so horrible as that wholesale slaughter could bring about any good, and yet there was something of a smoothing quality about even its baseness. There has never been such equality before or since such as that which the World War brought. Rich men fought by the side of paupers; poets swapped yarns with dry-goods salesmen, while Jews and Christians ate corned beef out of the same tin. Along with the general leveling influence came France's pardon of her prisoners in order that they might enter the army. Paul Watson became free and a French soldier. Because he was strong and had innate daring in his heart, he was placed in the aerial squad and cited many times for bravery. The close of the war gave him his place in French society as a hero. With only a memory of the war and an ugly scar on his left cheek, he took up his old life.

His firm resolutions about American white people still remained intact, and many chance encounters that followed the war are told from lip to lip proving that the war and his previous imprisonment had changed him little. He was the same Paul Watson to Montmartre as he shambled up rue Pigalle.

Rue Pigalle in the early evening has a somber beauty—gray as are most Paris streets and otherworldish. To those who know the district, it is the Harlem of Paris and rue Pigalle is its dusky Seventh Avenue. Most of the colored musicians that furnish Parisians and their visitors with entertainment live somewhere in the neighborhood of rue Pigalle. Sometime during every day each of these musicians makes a point of passing through rue Pigalle. Little wonder that almost any day will find Paul Watson going his shuffling way up the same street.

He reached the corner of rue de la Bruyere, and with sure instinct his feet stopped. Without half thinking he turned into "the Pit." Its full name is The Flea Pit. If you should ask one of the musicians why it was so called, he would answer you to the effect that it was called "the pit" because all the "fleas" hang out there. If you did not get the full Import of this explanation, he would go further and say that there were always "spades" in the pit, and they were as thick as fleas. Unless you could understand this latter attempt at clarity, you could not fully grasp what the Flea Pit means to the Negro musicians in Montmartre. It is a tiny cafe of the genus that is called *bistro* in France. Here the fiddle players, saxophone blowers, drumbeaters, and ivory ticklers gather at four in the afternoon for a porto or a game of billiards. Here the cabaret entertainers and supper musicians meet at one o'clock at night or thereafter for a whiskey and soda, or more billiards. Occasional sandwiches and a "quiet game" also play their parts in the popularity of the place. After a season or two it becomes a settled fact Just what time you may catch so-and-so at the famous "Pit."

The musicians were very fond of Paul and took particular delight in teasing him. He was one of the chosen few that all of the musicians conceded as being "regular." It was the pet Joke of the habitués of the cafe that Paul never bothered with girls. They always said that he could beat up ten men but was scared to death of one woman.

"Say fellow, when ya goin' a get hooked up?"

Can't say, Bo. Ain't so much on skirts."

"Man alive, ya don't know what you're missin'— somebody little and cute telling ya sweet things in your ear. Paris is full of women folks."

"I ain't much on 'em all the same. Then too, they're all white."

"What's it to ya? This ain't America."

"Can't help that. Get this—I'm colored, see? I ain't got nothing for no white meat to do. If a woman ever called me nigger, I'd have to kill her, that's all!"

"You for it, son. I can't give you a thing on this Mr. Jefferson way of lookin' at women."

"Oh, tain't that. I guess they're all right for those that wants 'em. Not me!"

"Oh, you ain't so forty. You'll fall like all the other spades I've ever seen. Your kind falls hardest."

And so Paul went his way—alone. He smoked and drank with the fellows and sat for hours in the Montmartre cafes and never knew the companionship of a woman. Then one night after his work he was walking along the street in his queer shuffling way when a woman stepped up to his side.

"*Voulez vous.*"

"Naw, go on away from here."

"Oh, you speak English, don't you?

"You an 'merican woman?"

"Used to be 'fore I went on the stage and got stranded over here."

"Well, get away from here. I don't like your kind!"

"Aw, Buddy, don't say that. I ain't prejudiced like some fool women."

"You don't know who I am, do you? I'm Paul Watson, and I hate American white folks, see?"

He pushed her aside and went on walking alone. e hadn't gone far when she caught up to him and said with sobs in her voice:—

"Oh, Lordy, please don't hate me 'cause I was born white and an American. I ain't got a penny to my name, and all the men pass me by cause I ain't spruced up Now you come along and won't look at me cause I'm white."

Paul strode along with her clinging to his arm. He tried to shake her off several times, but there was no use. She clung all the more desperately to him. He looked down at her frail body shaken with sobs, and something caught at his heart. Before he knew what he was doing he had said:— "Naw, I ain't that mean. I'll get you some grub. Quit your cryin'. Don't like seein' women folks cry."

It was the talk of Montmartre. Paul Watson takes a woman to Gavarnni's every night for dinner. He comes to the Flea Pit less frequently, thus giving the other musicians plenty of opportunity to discuss him.

"How times do change. Paul, the woman-hater, has a Jane now."

"You ain't said nothing, fella. That ain't all. She's white and an 'merican, too."

"That's the way with these spades. They beat up all the white men they can lay their hands on, but as soon as a gang of golden hair with blue eyes rubs up close to them they forget all they ever said about hatin' white folks."

"Guess he thinks that skirt's gone on him. Dumb fool!"

"Don't be no chineeman. That old gag don't fit for Paul He cain't understand it no more'n we can. Says he jus' can't help himself, every time she looks up into his eyes and asks him does he love her. They sure are happy together. Paul's goin to marry her, too. At first she kept saying that she didn't want to get married 'cause she wasn't the marrying kind and all that talk. Paul jus' laid down the law to her and told him he never would live with no woman without being married to her. Then she began to tell him all about her past life. He told her he didn't care nothing about what she used to be jus' so long as they loved each other now. Guess they'll make it."

"Yeah, Paul told me the same tale last night. He's sure gone on her all right."

"They're gettin' tied up next Sunday. So glad it's not me Don't trust these American dames. Me for the Frenchies."

"She ain't so worse for looks, Bud. Now that he's been furnishing the green for the rags."

"Yeah, but I don't see no reason for the wedding bell She was right—she ain't the marrying kind."

. . . And so Montmartre talked. In every cafe where the Negro musicians congregated, Paul Watson was the topic or conversation. He had suddenly fallen from his place as bronze God to almost less than the dust. The morning sun made queer patterns on Paul's sleeping face. He grimaced several times in his slumber, then finally half-opened his eyes. After a succession of dream-laden blinks he gave a great yawn and, rubbing his eyes, looked at the open window through which the sun shone brightly. His first conscious thought was that this was the bride's day and that bright sunshine prophesied happiness for the bride throughout her married life. His first impulse was to settle back into the covers and think drowsily about Mary and the queer twists life brings about, as is the wont of most bride grooms on their last morning of bachelorhood. He put this impulse aside in favor of dressing quickly and rushing downstairs to telephone to Mary to say "happy wedding day" to her.

One huge foot slipped into a worn bedroom slipper and then the other dragged painfully out of the warm bed were the courageous beginnings of his bridal toilette. With a look of triumph he put on his new gray suit that he had ordered from an English tailor. He carefully pulled a taffeta tie into place beneath his chin, noting as he looked at his face in the mirror that the scar he had received in the army was very ugly—funny, marrying an ugly man like him.

French telephones are such human faults. After trying for about fifteen minutes to get Central 32.01 he decided that he might as well walk around to Mary's hotel to give his greeting as to stand there in the lobby of his own, wasting his time. He debated this in his mind a great deal. They were to be married at four o'clock. It was eleven now, and it did seem a shame not to let her have a minute or two by herself. As he went walking down the street toward her hotel, he laughed to think of how one always cogitates over doing something and finally does the thing he wanted to in the beginning anyway.

Mud on his nice gray suit that the English tailor had made for him. Damn—gray suit—what did he have a gray suit on for, anyway. Folks with black faces shouldn't wear gray suits. God, but it was funny that time when he beat up that cracker at the Periquet. Fool couldn't shut his mouth he was so surprised. Crackers—damn 'em—he was one nigger that wasn't 'fraid of 'em. Wouldn't he have a hell of a time if he went back to America where black was black. Wasn't white nowhere, black wasn't. What was that thought he was trying to get ahold of—bumping around in his head— something he started to think about but couldn't remember it somehow.

The shrill whistle that is typical of the French subway pierced its way into his thoughts. Subway—why was he in the subway—he didn't want to go anyplace. He heard doors slamming and saw the blue uniforms of the conductors swinging on to the cars as the trains began to pull out of the station. With one or two strides he reached the last coach as it began to move up the platform. A bit out of breath he stood inside the train, and looking down at what he had in is hand, he saw that it was a tiny pink ticket. A first class ticket in a second class coach. The idea set him to laughing Everyone in the car turned and eyed him, but that did not bother him. Wonder what stop he'd get off— funny how these French said descend when they meant get off—funny he couldn't pick up French—been here so long. First class ticket in a second class coach!—that was one on him. Wedding day today, and that damn letter from Mary. How'd she say it now, "just couldn't go through with it," white women just don't marry colored men, and she was a street woman too. Why couldn't she have told him flat that she was just getting back on her feet at his expense. Funny that first class ticket he bought, wish he could see Mary—him a-going there to wish her "happy wedding day," too. Wonder what that French woman was looking at him so hard or. Guess it was the mud.

Sanctuary

by
NELLA LARSEN

ON THE SOUTHERN COAST, between Merton and Shawboro, there is a strip of desolation some half a mile wide and nearly ten miles long between the sea and old fields of ruined plantations. Skirting the edge of this narrow jungle is a partly grown-over road which still shows traces of furrows made by the wheels of wagons that have long since rotted away or been cut into firewood. This road is little used, now that the state has built its new highway a bit to the west and wagons are less numerous than automobiles.

In the forsaken road a man was walking swiftly. But in spite of his hurry, at every step he set down his feet with infinite care, for the night was windless and the heavy silence intensified each sound; even the breaking of a twig could be plainly heard. And the man had need of caution as well as haste.

Before a lonely cottage that shrank timidly back from the road, the man hesitated a moment, then struck out across the patch of green in front of it. Stepping behind a clump of bushes close to the house, he looked in through the lighted window at Annie Poole, standing at her kitchen table mixing the supper biscuits.

He was a big, black man with pale brown eyes in which there was an odd mixture of fear and amazement. The light showed streaks of gray soil on his heavy, sweating face and great hands, and on his torn clothes. In his woolly hair clung bits of dried leaves and dead grass.

He made a gesture as if to tap on the window, but turned away to the door instead. Without knocking he opened it and went in.

The woman's brown gaze was immediately on him, though she did not move. She said, "You ain't in no hurry, is you, Jim Hammer?" It wasn't, however, entirely a question.

"I'm in trouble, Miz Poole," the man explained, his voice shaking,
121

his fingers twitching.

"What you done done now?"

"Shot a man, Miz Poole."

"Truth?" The woman seemed calm. But the word was spat out.

"Yas'm. Shot him." In the man's tone was something of wonder, as if he himself could not quite believe that he had really done this thing which he affirmed.

"Dead?"

"Dunno, Miz Poole. dunno."

"White man or nigga?"

"Cain't say, Miz Poole. White man, I reckons."

Annie Poole looked at him with cold contempt. She was a tiny, withered woman—fifty perhaps—with a wrinkled face the color of old copper, framed by a crinkly mass of white hair. But about her small figure was some quality of hardness that belied her appearance of frailty. At last she spoke, boring her sharp little eyes into those of the anxious creature before her.

"An' what d'you want me to do 'bout it?"

"Jus' lemme stop till they've gone by. Hide me till they pass. Reckon they ain't far off now." His begging voice changed to a frightened whimper. "For de Lawd's sake, Miz Poole, lemme stop."

And why, the woman inquired caustically, should she run the dangerous risk of hiding him?

"Obadiah, he'd lemme stop if he was to home," the man whined.

Annie Poole sighed. "Yes," she admitted, slowly, reluctantly, "I spec' he would. Obadiah, he's too good to all you no 'count trash." Her slight shoulders lifted in a hopeless shrug. "Yes, I reckon he'd do it. Especially seein how he always set such a heap of store by you. Cain't see what for, myself. I sure don't see nothing in you but a heap of dirt."

But a look of irony, of cunning, of complicity passed over her face. She went on, "Still, considering all an' all, how Obadaiah's right fond of you, an' how white folks is white folks, I'm a-gwine hide you dis one time."

Crossing the kitchen, she opened a door leading into a small bedroom, saying, "Git yourself in dat feather bed an I'm a-gwine put de clothes on de top. Don't reckon they'll fin you if they look for you in my house. An I don't spec' they'll go for to do dat. Not lessen you been careless an let 'em track you here." She turned on him a withering look. "But you always been triflin'. Cain't do nothing proper. An' I'm a-tellin' you if they weren't white folks an you a poor nigga, I

122

sure wouldn't be lettin' you mess up my feather bed dis evenin', 'cause I jes' plain don't want you here. I done kept myself outta trouble all my life. So's Obadaiah."

"I'm mighty 'bliged to you, Miz Poole. You sure am one good oman. De Lawd'll most certainly—"

Annie Poole cut him off. "Dis ain't no time for all dat kinda fiddle-de-roll. I does my duty as I sees it without no thanks from you. If de Lord had given you a white face 'stead of dat black one, I sure would turn you out. Now hush your mouth an' git yourself in. An' don't git movin' and scrunchin' under those covers and git yourself caught in my house."

Without further comment the man did as he was told er he had laid his soiled body and grimy garments between her snowy sheets, Annie Poole carefully rearranged the covering and placed piles of freshly laundered linen on op. en she gave a pat here and there, eyed the result, and finding it satisfactory, went back to her cooking.

Jim Hammer settled down to the racking business of waiting until the approaching danger should have passed him by. Soon savory odors seeped in to him, and he realized that he was hungry. He wished that Annie Poole would bring him something to eat. Just one biscuit. But she wouldn't, he knew. Not she. She was a hard one, Obadiah s mother.

By and by he fell into a sleep, from which he was dragged back by the rumbling sound of wheels in the road outside. For a second fear clutched so tightly at him that he almost leaped from the suffocating shelter of the bed m order to make some active attempt to escape the horror that his capture meant. There was a spasm at his heart, a pain so sharp, so slashing that he had to suppress an impulse to cry out. He felt himself falling. Down, down, down ... Everything grew dim and very distant in his memory ... vanished ... came rushing back.

Outside there was silence. He strained his ears. Nothing. No footsteps. No voices. They had gone on then. Gone without even stopping to ask Annie Poole if she had seen him pass that way. A sigh of relief slipped from him. His thick lips curled in an ugly, cunning smile; It had been smart of him to think of coming to Obadiah s mother s to hide. She was an old demon, but he was safe in her house.

He lay a short while longer listening intently and, hearing nothing, started to get up. But immediately he stopped, his yellow eyes glowing like pale flames. He had heard the unmistakable sound of men coming toward the house. Swiftly he slid back into the heavy, hot stuffiness of the bed and lay listening fearfully.

The terrifying sounds drew nearer. Slowly. Heavily. Just for a moment he thought they were not coming in—they took so long. But there was a light knock and the noise of a door being opened. His whole body went taut. His feet felt frozen, his hands clammy, his tongue like a weighted, dying thing. His pounding heart made it hard for his straining ears to hear what they were saying out there.

"Evenin', Mistah Lowndes." Annie Poole's voice sounded as it always did, sharp and dry.

There was no answer. Or had he missed it? With great care he shifted his position, bringing his head nearer the edge of the bed. Still he heard nothing. What were they waiting for? Why didn't they ask about him?

Annie Poole, it seemed, was of the same mind. "I don't reckon you done traipsed 'way out here jes' for nothing," she hinted.

"There's bad news for you, Annie, I'm 'fraid." The sheriff's voice was low and queer.

Jim Hammer visualized him standing out there—a tall stooped man, his white tobacco-stained mustache drooping Imply at the ends, his nose hooked and sharp, his eyes blue an cold. Bill Lowndes was a hard one too. And white.

"What bad news, Mistah Lowndes?" The woman put the question quietly, directly.

"Obadiah—" The sheriff began—hesitated—began again. Obadiah—ah—er he's outside, Annie. I'm 'fraid—"

"Shucks! You done missed. Obadiah, he ain't done nothing, Mistah Lowndes; Obadiah!" she called stridently. "Obadaiah, git here an' explain yourself."

But Obadiah didn't answer, didn't come in. Other men came in. Came in with steps that dragged and halted. No one spoke. Not even Annie Poole. Something was laid carefully upon the floor.

"Obadiah, chile," his mother said softly, "Obadiah, chile. Then, with sudden alarm, "He ain't dead, is he? Mistah Lowndes! Obadiah, he ain't dead?"

Jim Hammer didn't catch the answer to that pleading question. A new fear was stealing over him.

"There was a to-do, Annie," Bill Lowndes explained gently, at the garage back of the factory. Fellow tryin' to steal tires. Obadiah heard a noise an' run out with two or three others. Scared the rascal all right. Fired off his gun n run. We allow it to be Jim Hammer. Picked up his cap back there. Never was no 'count. Thievin' an' sly. But we'll git him, Annie. We'll git him."

The man huddled in the feather bed prayed silently. "Oh Lord! I didn't go to do it. Not Obadiah, Lord. You knows dat. You knows it. And into his frenzied brain came the thought that it would be better for him to get up and go out to them before Annie Poole gave him away. For he was lost now. With all his great strength he tried to get himself out of the bed. But he couldn't.

"Oh Lord!" he moaned. "Oh Lord!" His thoughts were bitter, and they ran through his mind like panic. He knew that it had come to pass as it said somewhere in the Bible about the wicked. The Lord had stretched out his hand and smitten him. He was paralyzed. He couldn't move hand or foot. He moaned again. It was all there was left for him to do. For in the terror of this new calamity that had come upon him, he had forgotten the waiting danger which was so near out there in the kitchen.

His hunters, however, didn't hear him. Bill Lowndes was saying, "We been a-lookin' for Jim out along the old road. Figured he'd make tracks for Shawboro. You ain't noticed anybody pass this evenin', Annie?"

The reply came promptly, unwaveringly. No, I ain't sees nobody pass. Not yet."

Jim Hammer caught his breath.

"Well," the sheriff concluded, "we'll be gittin' along. Obadiah was a mighty fine boy. If they was all like him—. I'm sorry, Annie. Anything I can do let me know.

"Thank you, Mistah Lowndes."

With the sound of the door closing on the departing men, power to move came back to the man in the bedroom. He pushed his dirt-caked feet out from the covers and rose up, but crouched down again. He wasn't cold now, but hot all over and burning. Almost he wished that Bill Lowndes and his men had taken him with them.

Annie Poole had come into the room.

It seemed a long time before Obadiah's mother spoke. When she did, there were no tears, no reproaches; but there was a raging fury in her voice as she lashed out, it outta my feather bed, Jim Hammer, an outta ma house, an' don't nevah stop thanking your Jesus for giving you dat black face."

All That Hair

by
MELISSA LINN

SEVEN-YEAR-OLD MINNIE MAE looked longingly at the side-walk as she walked from school to her mother's place of work. It was noon. Several little girls passed her without so much as a hello. Minnie Mae knew why they ignored her. She wasn't like them. She didn't have the right kind of hair.

More than anything else in this world, Minnie Mae wanted pretty curly hair crowned by a stiff pink butterfly bow. All the little girls in her room at school had soft, silken, flexible locks, and from her seat in the rear of the room she could look over the room and see all the smooth heads: brown, yellow, black, and red. All of them topped by pink, blue, plaid, or yellow butterfly bows. They were just simply beautiful. Oh, if only she could run a comb through her hair as non-chalantly as Sally Lou and have it leave little rows where the teeth had been! Or to have it fall down into her eyes when she stooped over, or to run in the wind and have it blow before her eyes. But no, she must have these inky stiff naps that made her cry every time her mother washed them. If only a fairy would come and change her like she did Cinderella! Maybe a fairy would. So Minnie Mae dreamed on as she walked slowly toward the white folks' house where her mother worked and where she ate her lunch every day.

Ever since she could remember she had been going to Mrs. Whitham's to see Mama. Once Mama dressed her up, and she was presented to Mrs. Whitham to speak her Easter piece, then Mrs. Whitham gave her cookies and fifty cents for her new pocketbook. Mrs. Whitham was awfully nice—she was little, almost as little as Minnie Mae. She looked just like a china doll. Her hair was light and curled all over her head in tiny, silken curls. But Mama told Aunt Joe that Mrs. Whitham's hair was false, just like the wigs you wore on Halloween.

Minnie Mae turned up a broad white driveway and followed it around to the back door. She opened a screen door softly and stepped into a clean white kitchen. It was empty. She went on through to the stairs and started softly up. Mama was probably making up the beds, and perhaps she would let her help.

On reaching the top of the stairs, Minnie Mae peered into the first bedroom. It was empty. She tiptoed to the second room and stopped, for there lay Mrs. Whitham, sound asleep. Minnie Mae knew she was asleep, because her eyes were shut and her mouth, hanging loosely open, allowed a thin trickle of saliva to escape and roll down to the pillow. Minnie Mae stared with wide eyes at the white lady because her head was as smooth and shiny as her little baby brother's. It looked just like a new potato that mother had scraped very carefully in order to cream whole

Close by, on the dresser, where its owner had placed it in order to relieve an aching head, was the wig of beautiful hair, the silken curls shining in the sun. When Minnie Mae saw it, her eyes grew big and she began to breathe harder. If she could just try it on. Oh, if she just dared. She looked again at the sleeping lady, then stepped softly across the room, picked up the wig, and placed it gently on her head.

She looked into the mirror and saw a transformed creature. The inch-long, stubborn, greasy kinks were gone, and silk curls tumbled profusely in their place. Oh, if only she could wear it to school! The kids would like her then. She gave one look at the sleeping lady, then turned and ran quickly out of the room and down the stairs. She stopped. Mama! Where was she? Then she heard a slow boop-a-boop-aboop-aboop— and she knew her mother was washing in the basement. She picked up a piece of cake from the table and ran out of the door. She ran all the way to school, holding the wig on with one hand and thinking all the time. Now maybe Mary Lou, that pretty little fat girl, would play with her at recess. Maybe all the girls, Sally Jane, Lillian, and Ruth, would come and ask her to play jack-stones. Maybe they'd even ask her to come over to their houses after school and play "grown-up." Carried away by her realistic dream, her heart bounded in delightful anticipation, and she reached the school and ran up the steps and into her room.

At first the teacher didn't see her. Then, as a surreptitious tittering arose and gradually grew to open snickering and suppressed laughter, she looked up, frowning. As her eyes focused-on Minnie Mae, they widened with incredulity, her large mouth fell open, and red splotches began to spread slowly on her coarse neck. And then the little brown girl, whom class and teacher alike had ignored all year, was suddenly the amused and contemptuous center of attraction.

The child stopped, dismayed. Her eyes, grown enormous, stared in horror and fright from under the white wig. The sound of laughter roared in her ears, and as her heart began to pound with misgivings, the teacher's strident voice cried, "You! Come here!"

At the sound of the angry voice, the laughter ceased, and it was very quiet in the room. Minnie Mae felt the whole sea of white faces staring, mocking, burning her. Laughing at her. Suddenly everything became blurred, and a greater panic seized upon her, for she felt a wet scalding run down her legs and, to her horror and shame, saw a puddle grow as big as a river at her feet and start rolling down the aisle, under the seats, a long, wide condemning river. They would never like her now!

Shame mingled with the fright, and tears came. Despairing sobs rose in her throat, and she burst into uncontrollable crying. Loud, racking sobs shook her body, and she stood rooted to the spot, her stockings clinging cold and wet to her legs. She bowed her head in the crook of her arm, and the sobs made the absurd white curls of Mrs. Whitham's wig jiggle precariously on the little brown head.

Annoyed and contemptuous, the teacher strode down the aisle, pushed the child into the cloak room, and demanded, "Where did you get that hair?" Minnie Mae was sobbing so much, she couldn't answer, whereupon the teacher half pushed, half shoved her down to the principal's office. That buxom lady gave a glance at the mournful brown girl, her eyes took in the wet soaked stockings, and she told her to go home.

Minnie Mae, crying as though her heart would burst, ran into her mother's place of work, and when that good woman saw her child come in wearing her employer's hair, her heart jumped violently.

"God a'mighty, Minnie Mae . . . here—"

Without another word she snatched the wig from the child's head, hastened quick and soft as a cat upstairs where her mistress was still sleeping, and put the wig back in its proper place, then descended rapidly, and shaking the child violently, she whispered fiercely, "Hm! Do you want to wake Mrs. Whitham and have her find out you've had her wig, so I'll lose my job? Where would we be then?" She released the child and said, "You go on home, and I'll tend to you tonight after work." She gave the child a shove out the door and turned back to her work, cooking food. She muttered, "Children sure are more bother than they are worth, always doing something to upset folks.

Minnie Mae went slowly out the door, toward her home, and as she walked along in the warm afternoon sun, long shuddering sighs escaped from her heart. By the time she had finished the long walk home, the sighs had stopped, but a new wisdom and sadness was buried deep in a brown child's heart.

Our Nig

by

HARRIET E. WILSON

Preface

In offering to the public the following pages, the writer confesses her inability to minister to the refined and cultivated, the pleasure supplied by more able pens. It is not for such these crude narrations appear. Deserted by kindred, disabled by failing health, I am forced to some experiment which shall aid me in maintaining myself and child without extinguishing this feeble life. I would not from these motives even palliate slavery at the South, by disclosures of its appurtenances North. My mistress was wholly imbued with southern principles. I do not pretend to divulge every transaction in my own life, which the unprejudiced would declare unfavourable in comparison with treatment of legal bondmen; I have purposely omitted what would most provoke shame in our good anti-slavery friends at home.

My humble position and frank confession of errors will, I hope, shield me from severe criticism. Indeed, defects are so apparent it requires no skillful hand to expose them.

I sincerely appeal to my coloured brethren universally for patronage, hoping they will not condemn this attempt of their sister to be erudite, but rally around me a faithful band of supporters and defenders.

H.E.W

LONELY MAG SMITH! See her as she walks with downcast eyes and heavy heart. It was not always thus. She had a loving, trusting heart. Early deprived of parental guardianship, far removed from relatives, she was left to guide her tiny boat over life's surges alone and inexperienced. As she merged into womanhood, unprotected, uncherished, uncared for, there fell on her ear the music of love, awakening an intensity of emotion long dormant. It whispered of an elevation previously unaspired to; of ease and plenty her simple heart had never dreamed of as hers. She knew the voice of her charmer, so ravishing, sounded far above her. It seemed like an angel's, alluring her upward and onward. She thought she could ascend to him and become an equal. She surrendered to him a price-less gem, which he proudly garnered as a trophy, with those of other victims, and left her to her fate. The world seemed full of hateful deceivers and crushing arrogance. Conscious that the great bond of union to her former companions was severed, that the disdain of oth-ers would be insupportable, she determined to leave the few friends she possessed, and seek an asylum among strangers. Her offspring came unwelcomed, and before its nativity numbered weeks, it passed from earth, ascending to a purer and better life.

"God be thanked," ejaculated Mag, as she saw its breathing cease; "no one can taunt her with my ruin."

Blessed release! may we all respond. How many pure, innocent children not only inherit a wicked heart of their own, claiming life-long scrutiny and restraint, but are heirs also of parental disgrace and calumny, from which only long years of patient endurance in paths of rectitude can disencumber them.

Mag's new home was soon contaminated by the publicity of her fall; she had a feeling of degradation oppressing her; but she resolved to be circumspect, and try to regain in a measure what she had lost. Then some foul tongue would jest of her shame, and averted looks and cold greetings disheartened her. She saw she could not bury in forgetfulness her misdeed, so she resolved to leave her home and seek another in the place she at first fled from.

Alas, how fearful are we to be first in extending a helping hand to those who stagger in the mires of infamy; to speak the first words of hope and warning to those emerging into the sunlight of morality! Who can tell what numbers, advancing just far enough to hear a cold welcome and join in the reserved converse of professed reformers, disappointed, disheartened, have chosen to dwell in unclean places, rather than encounter these "holier-than-thou" of the great brother-hood of man!

Such was Mag's experience; and disdaining to ask favour or friendship from a sneering world, she resolved to shut herself up in a hovel she had often passed in better days, and which she knew to be untenanted. She vowed to ask no favours of familiar faces; to die neglected and forgotten before she would be dependent on any. Removed from the village, she was seldom seen except as upon your introduction, gentle reader, with downcast visage, returning her work to her employer, and thus providing herself with the means of subsistence. In two years many hands craved the same avocation; foreigners who cheapened toil and clamoured for a livelihood, competed with her, and she could not thus sustain herself. She was now above no drudgery. Occasionally old acquaintances called to be favoured with help of some kind, which she was glad to bestow for the sake of the money it would bring her; but the association with them was such a painful reminder of bygones, she returned to her hut morose and revengeful, refusing all offers of a better home than she possessed. Thus she lived for years, hugging her wrongs, but making no effort to escape. She had never known plenty, scarcely competency; but the present was beyond comparison with those innocent years when the coronet of virtue was hers.

Every year her melancholy increased, her means diminished. At last no one seemed to notice her, save a kind-hearted African, who often called to inquire after her health and to see if she needed any fuel, he having the responsibility of furnishing that article, and she in return mending or making garments.

"How much you earn this week, Mag?" asked he one Saturday evening.

"Little enough, Jim. Two or three days without any dinner. I washed for the Reeds, and did a small job for Mrs. Bellmont; that's all. I shall starve soon, unless I can get more to do. Folks seem as afraid to come here as if they expected to get some awful disease. I don't believe there is a person in the world but would be glad to have me dead and out of the way."

"No, no, Mag! don't talk so. You shan't starve so long as I have barrels to hoop. Peter Greene boards me cheap. I'll help you, if nobody else will."

A tear stood in Mag's faded eye. "I'm glad," she said, with a softer tone than before, "if there is *one* who isn't glad to see me suffer. I believe all Singleton wants to see me punished, and feel as if they could tell when I've been punished long enough. It's a long day ahead they'll set it, I reckon."

After the usual supply of fuel was prepared, Jim returned home. Full of pity for Mag, he set about devising measures for her relief. "By golly!" said he to himself one day—for he had become so absorbed in Mag's interest that he had fallen into a habit of musing aloud —"By golly! I wish she'd marry me."

"Who?" shouted Pete Greene, suddenly starting from an unobserved corner of the rude shop.

"Where you come from, you sly nigger!" exclaimed Jim.

"Come, tell me, who is it?" said Pete; a Mag Smith, you want to marry?"

"Git out, Pete! and when you come in this shop again, let a nigger know it. Don't steal in like a thief."

Pity and love know little severance. One attends the other. Jim acknowledged the presence of the former, and his efforts on Mag's behalf told also of a finer principle.

This sudden expedient which he had unintentionally disclosed, roused his thinking and inventive powers to study upon the best method of introducing the subject to Mag.

He belted his barrels, with many a scheme revolving in his mind, none of which quite satisfied him, or seemed, on the whole, expedient. He thought of the pleasing contrast between her fair face and his own dark skin; the smooth, straight hair, which he had once, in expression of pity, kindly stroked on her now wrinkled but once fair brow. There was a tempest gathering in his heart, and at last, to ease his pent-up passion, he exclaimed aloud, "By golly!" Recollecting his former exposure, he glanced around to see if Pete was in hearing again. Satisfied on this point, he continued: "She'd be as much of a prize to me as she'd fall short of coming up to the mark with white folks. I don't care for past things. I've done things 'fore now I'm 'shamed of. She's good enough for me, any how."

One more glance about the premises to be sure Pete was away.

The next Saturday night brought Jim to the hovel again. The cold was fast coming to tarry its apportioned time. Mag was nearly despairing of meeting its rigor.

"How's the wood, Mag?" asked Jim.

"All gone; and no more to cut, any how," was the reply.

"Too bad!" Jim said. His truthful reply would have been, I'm glad.

"Anything to eat in the house?" continued he.

"No," replied Mag.

"Too bad!" again, orally, with the same inward gratification as before.

"Well, Mag," said Jim, after a short pause, "you're down low enough. I don't see but I've got to take care of you. S'posin' we marry!"

Mag raised her eyes, full of amazement, and uttered a sonorous

"What?"

Jim felt abashed for a moment. He knew well what were her objections.

"You've had experience of white folks, any how. They run off and left you, and now none of 'em come near you to see if you're dead or alive. I'm black outside, I know, but I've got a white heart inside. Which you rather have, a black heart in a white skin, or a white heart in a black one?"

"Oh, dear!" sighed Mag; "Nobody on earth cares for me—"

"I do," interrupted Jim.

"I can do but two things," said she, "beg my living, or get it from you."

"Take me, Mag. I can give you a better home than this, and not let you suffer so."

He prevailed; they married. You can philosophize, gentle reader, upon the impropriety of such unions, and preach dozens of sermons on the evils of amalgamation. Want is a more powerful philosopher and preacher. Poor Mag. She has sundered another bond which held her to her fellows. She has descended another step down the ladder of infamy.

JIM, PROUD OF his treasure —a white wife—tried hard to fulfill his promises; and furnished her with a more comfortable dwelling, diet, and apparel. It was comparatively a comfortable winter she passed after her marriage. When Jim could work, all went on well. Industrious, and fond of Mag, he was determined she should not regret her union to him. Time levied an additional charge upon him, in the form of two pretty mulattos, whose infantile pranks amply repaid the additional toil. A few years, and a severe cough and pain in his side compelled him to be an idler for weeks together, and Mag had thus a reminder of bygones. She cared for him only as a means to subserve her own comfort; yet she nursed him faithfully and true to marriage vows till death released her. He became the victim of consumption. He loved Mag to the last. So long as life continued, he stifled his sensibility to pain, and toiled for her sustenance long after he was able to do so.

A few expressive wishes for her welfare; a hope of better days for her; an anxiety lest they should not all go to the "good place;" brief advice about their children; a hope expressed that Mag would not be neglected as she used to be; the manifestation of Christian patience;

these were *all* the legacy of miserable Mag. A feeling of cold desolation came over her, as she turned from the grave of one who had been truly faithful to her.

She was now expelled from companionship with white people; this last step—her union with a black—was the climax of repulsion.

Seth Shipley, a partner in Jim's business, wished her to remain in her present home; but she declined, and returned to her hovel again, with obstacles threefold more insurmountable than before. Seth accompanied her, giving her a weekly allowance which furnished most of the food necessary for the four inmates. After a time, work failed; their means were reduced.

How Mag toiled and suffered, yielding to fits of desperation, bursts of anger, and uttering curses too fearful to repeat. When both were supplied with work, they prospered; if idle, they were hungry together. In this way their interests became united; they planned for the future together. Mag had lived an outcast for years. She had ceased to feel the gushings of penitence; she had crushed the sharp agonies of an awakened conscience. She had no longings for a purer heart, a better life. Far easier to descend lower. She entered the darkness of perpetual infamy. She asked not the rite of civilization or Christianity. Her will made her the wife of Seth. Soon followed scenes familiar and trying.

"It's no use," said Seth one day; "we must give the children away, and try to get work in some other place."

"Who'll take the black devils?" snarled Mag.

"They're none of mine," said Seth; "what you growling about?"

"Nobody will want any thing of mine, or yours either," she replied.

"We'll make 'em, perhaps," he said. "There's Frado, six years old and pretty, even white folks'll say so. She'd be a prize somewhere," he continued, tipping his chair back against the wall, and placing his feet upon the rounds, as if he had much more to say when in the right position.

Frado, as they called one of Mag's children, was a beautiful mulatto, with long, curly black hair, and handsome, roguish eyes, sparkling with an exuberance of spirit almost beyond restraint.

Hearing her name mentioned, she looked up from her play, to see what Seth had to say of her.

"Wouldn't the Bellmonts take her?" asked Seth.

"Bellmonts?" shouted Mag. "His wife is a right she-devil! and if—

"Hadn't they better be all together?" interrupted Seth, reminding her of a like epithet used in reference to her little ones.

Without seeming to notice him, she continued, "She can't keep a girl in the house over a week; and Mr. Bellmont wants to hire a boy to work for him, but he can't find one that will live in the house with her; she's so ugly, they can't."

"Well, we've got to make a move soon," answered Seth; "if you go with me, we shall go right off. Had you rather spare the other one?" asked Seth, after a short pause.

"One's as bad as the other," replied Mag. "Frado is such a wild thing, and means to do jest as she's a mind to; she won't go if she don't want to. I don't want to tell her she is to be given away."

"I will," said Seth. "Come here, Frado?"

The child seemed to have some dim foreshadowing of evil, and declined.

"Come here," he continued; "I want to tell you something."

She came reluctantly. He took her hand and said: "We're going to move, by-'m-bye; will you go?"

"No!" screamed she; and giving a sudden jerk which destroyed Seth's equilibrium, left him sprawling on the floor, while she escaped through the open door.

"She's a hard one," said Seth, brushing his patched coat sleeve. "I'd risk her at Bellmont's."

They discussed the expediency of a speedy departure. Seth would first seek employment, and then return for Mag. They would take with them what they could carry, and leave the rest with Pete Greene, and come for them when they were wanted. They were long in arranging affairs satisfactorily, and were not a little startled at the close of their conference to find Frado missing. They thought approaching night would bring her. Twilight passed into darkness, and she did not come. They thought she had understood their plans, and had, perhaps, permanently withdrawn. They could not rest without making some effort to ascertain her retreat. Seth went in pursuit, and returned without her. They rallied others when they discovered that another little coloured girl was missing, a favourite playmate of Frado's. All effort proved unavailing. Mag felt sure her fears were realised, and that she might never see her again. Before her anxieties became realities, both were safely returned, and from them and their attendant they learned that they went to walk, and not minding the direction soon found themselves lost. They had climbed fences and walls, passed through thickets and marshes, and when night approached selected a thick cluster of shrubbery as a covert for the night. They were discovered by the person who now restored them, chatting of their prospects, Frado attempting to banish the childish fears of her companion. As they were some miles from home, they were kindly cared for until morning. Mag was relieved to know her child was not driven to desperation by their intentions to relieve themselves of her, and she was inclined to think severe restraint would be healthful.

The removal was all arranged; the few days necessary for such migrations passed quickly, and one bright summer morning they bade farewell to their Singleton hovel, and with budgets and bundles commenced their weary march. As they neared the village, they heard the merry shouts of children gathered around the schoolroom, awaiting the coming of their teacher.

"Halloo!" screamed one, "Black, white and yeller!" "Black, white and yeller," echoed a dozen voices.

It did not grate so harshly on poor Mag as once it would. She did not even turn her head to look at them. She had passed into an insensibility no childish taunt could penetrate, else she would have reproached herself as she passed familiar scenes, for extending the separation once so easily annihilated by steadfast integrity. Two miles beyond lived the Bellmonts, in a large, old fashioned, two-storey white house, surrounded by fruitful acres, and embellished by shrubbery and shade trees. Years ago a youthful couple consecrated it as home; and after many little feet had worn paths to favourite fruit trees, and over its green hills, and mingled at last with brother man in the race which belongs neither to the swift or strong, the sire became grey-haired and decrepit, and went to his last repose. His aged consort soon followed him. The old homestead thus passed into the hands of a son, to whose wife Mag had applied the epithet "she-devil," as may be remembered. John, the son, had not in his family arrangements departed from the example of the father. The pastimes of his boyhood were ever freshly revived by witnessing the games of his own sons as they rallied about the same goal his youthful feet had often won; as well as by the amusements of his daughters in their imitations of maternal duties.

At the time we introduce them, however, John is wearing the badge of age. Most of his children were from home; some seeking employment; some were already settled in homes of their own. A maiden sister shared with him the estate on which he resided, and occupied a portion of the house.

Within sight of the house, Seth seated himself with his bundles and the child he had been leading, while Mag walked onward to the house leading Frado. A knock at the door brought Mrs. Bellmont, and Mag asked if she would be willing to let that child stop there while she went to the Reed's house to wash, and when she came back she would call and get her. It seemed a novel request, but she consented.

Why the impetuous child entered the house, we cannot tell; the door closed, and Mag hastily departed. Frado waited for the close of day, which was to bring back her mother. Alas! it never came. It was the last time she ever saw or heard of her mother.

AS THE DAY closed and Mag did not appear, surmises were expressed by the family that she never intended to return. Mr. Bellmont was a kind, humane man, who would not grudge hospitality to the poorest wanderer, nor fail to sympathize with any sufferer, however humble. The child's desertion by her mother appealed to his sympathy, and he felt inclined to succour her. To do this in opposition to Mrs. Bellmont's wishes, would be like encountering a whirlwind charged with fire, daggers and spikes. She was not as susceptible of fine emotions as her spouse. Mag's opinion of her was not without foundation. She was self-willed, haughty, undisciplined, arbitrary and severe. In common parlance, she was a *scold*, a thorough one. Mr. B. remained silent during the consultation which follows, engaged in by mother, Mary and John, or Jack, as he was familiarly called.

"Send her to the County House," said Mary, in reply to the query what should be done with her, in a tone which indicated self-importance in the speaker. She was indeed the idol of her mother, and more nearly resembled her in disposition and manners than the others.

Jane, an invalid daughter, the eldest of those at home, was reclining on a sofa apparently uninterested.

"Keep her," said Jack. "She's real handsome and bright, and not very black, either."

"Yes," rejoined Mary; that's just like you, Jack. She'll be of no use at all these three years, right under foot all the time."

"Poh! Miss Mary; if she should stay, it wouldn't be two days before you would be telling the girls about *our* nig, *our* nig!" retorted Jack.

"I don't want a nigger 'round me, do you, mother?" asked Mary.

"I don't mind the nigger in the child. I should like a dozen better

138

than one," replied her mother. "If I could make her do my work in a few years, I would keep her. I have so much trouble with girls I hire, I am almost persuaded if I have one to train up in my way from a child, I shall be able to keep them awhile. I am tired of changing every few months."

Where could she sleep?" asked Mary. "I don't want her near me."

"In the L chamber," answered the mother.

"How'll she get there?" asked Jack. "She'll be afraid to go through that dark passage, and she can't climb the ladder safely."

"She'll have to go there; it's good enough for a nigger," was the reply.

Jack was sent on horseback to ascertain if Mag was at her home. He returned with the testimony of Pete Greene that they were fairly departed, and that the child was intentionally thrust upon their family.

The imposition was not at all relished by Mrs. B., or the pert, haughty Mary, who had just glided into her teens.

"Show the child to bed, Jack," said his mother. You seem most pleased with the little nigger, so you may introduce her to her room."

He went to the kitchen, and, taking Frado gently by the hand, told her he would put her in bed now; perhaps her mother would come the next night after her.

It was not yet quite dark, so they ascended the stairs without any light, passing through nicely furnished rooms, which were a source of great amazement to the child. He opened the door which connected with her room by a dark, unfinished passage-way. "Don't bump your head," said Jack, and stepped before to open the door leading into her apartment,—an unfinished chamber over the kitchen, the roof slanting nearly to the floor, so that the bed could stand only in the middle of the room. A small half window furnished light and air. Jack returned to the sitting room with the remark that the child would soon outgrow those quarters.

"When she *does*, she'll outgrow the house," remarked the mother.

"What can she do to help you?" asked Mary. "She came just in the right time, didn't she? Just the very day after Bridget left," continued she.

"I'll see what she can do in the morning," was the answer.

While this conversation was passing below, Frado lay, revolving in her little mind whether she would remain or not until her mother's return. She was of willful, determined nature, a stranger to fear, and would not hesitate to wander away should she decide to. She

139

remembered the conversation of her mother with Seth, the words "given away" which she heard used in reference to herself; and though she did not know their full import, she thought she should, by remaining, be in some relation to white people she was never favoured with before. So she resolved to tarry, with the hope that mother would come and get her some time. The hot sun had penetrated her room, and it was long before a cooling breeze reduced the temperature so that she could sleep.

Frado was called early in the morning by her new mistress. Her first work was to feed the hens. She was shown how it was *always* to be done, any departure from this rule to be punished by a whipping. She was then accompanied by Jack to drive the cows to pasture, so she might learn the way. Upon her return she was allowed to eat her breakfast, consisting of a bowl of skimmed milk, with brown bread crusts, which she was told to eat, standing, by the kitchen table, and must not be over ten minutes about it. Meanwhile the family were taking their morning meal in the dining-room. This over, she was placed on a cricket to wash the common dishes; she was to be in waiting always to bring wood and chips, to run hither and thither from room to room.

A large amount of dish-washing for small hands followed dinner. Then the same after tea and going after the cows finished her first day's work. It was a new discipline to the child. She found some attractions about the place, and she retired to rest at night more willing to remain. The same routine followed day after day, with slight variation; adding a little more work, and spicing the toil with "words that burn," and frequent blows on her head. These were great annoyances to Frado, and had she known where her mother was, she would have gone at once to her. She was often greatly wearied, and silently wept over her sad fate. At first she wept aloud, which Mrs. Bellmont noticed by applying a rawhide, always at hand in the kitchen. It was a symptom of discontent and complaining which must be "nipped in the bud," she said.

Thus passed a year. No intelligence of Mag. It was now certain Frado was to become a permanent member of the family. Her labours were multiplied; she was quite indispensable, although but seven years old. She had never learned to read, never heard of a school until her residence in the family.

Mrs. Bellmont was in doubt about the utility of attempting to educate people of colour, who were incapable of elevation. This subject occasioned a lengthy discussion in the family. Mr. Bellmont, Jane and

140

Jack arguing for Frado's education; Mary and her mother objecting. At last Mr. Bellmont declared decisively that she *should* go to school. He was a man who seldom decided controversies at home. The word once spoken admitted of no appeal; so, notwithstanding Mary's objection that she would have to attend the same school she did, the word became law.

It was to be a new scene to Frado, and Jack had many queries and conjectures to answer. He was himself too far advanced to attend the summer school, which Frado regretted, having had too many opportunities of witnessing Miss Mary's temper to feel safe in her company alone.

The opening day of school came. Frado sauntered on far in the rear of Mary, who was ashamed to be seen "walking with a nigger." As soon as she appeared, with scanty clothing and bared feet, the children assembled, noisily published her approach: "See that nigger," shouted one. "Look! look!" cried another. "I won't play with her," said one little girl. "Nor I neither," replied another.

Mary evidently relished these sharp attacks, and saw a fair prospect of lowering Nig where, according to her views, she belonged. Poor Frado, chagrined and grieved, felt that her anticipations of pleasure at such a place were far from being realised. She was just deciding to return home, and never come there again, when the teacher appeared, and observing the downcast looks of the child, took her by the hand, and led her into the school-room. All followed, and, after the bustle of securing seats was over, Miss Marsh inquired if the children knew "any cause for the sorrow of that little girl?" pointing to Frado. It was soon all told. She then reminded them of their duties to the poor and friendless; their cowardice in attacking a young innocent child; referred them to one who looks not on outward appearances, but on the heart. "She looks like a good girl; I think I shall love her, so lay aside all prejudice, and vie with each other in showing kindness and good-will to one who seems different from you," were the closing remarks of the kind lady. Those kind words! The most agreeable sound which ever meets the ear of sorrowing, grieving childhood.

Example rendered her words efficacious. Day by day there was a manifest change of deportment towards "Nig." Her speeches often drew merriment from the children; no one could do more to enliven their favourite pastimes than Frado. Mary could not endure to see her thus noticed, yet knew not how to prevent it. She could not influence her schoolmates as she wished. She had not gained their affections by winning ways and yielding points of controversy. On the contrary, she was self-willed, domineering; every day reported "mad" by some of her companions. She availed herself of the only alternative, abuse and taunts, as they returned from school. This was not satisfactory; she wanted to use physical force "to subdue her," to "keep her down." There was, on their way home, a field intersected by a stream over which a single plank was placed for a crossing. It occurred to Mary that it would be a punishment to Nig to compel her to cross over; so she dragged her to the edge, and told her authoritatively to go over. Nig hesitated, resisted. Mary placed herself behind the child, and, in the struggle to force her over, lost her footing and plunged into the stream. Some of the larger scholars being in sight, ran, and thus prevented Mary from drowning and Frado from falling. Nig scampered home fast as possible, and Mary went to the nearest house, dripping, to procure a change of garments. She came loitering home, half crying, exclaiming, "Nig pushed me into the stream!" She then related the particulars. Nig was called from the kitchen. Mary stood with anger flashing in her eyes. Mr. Bellmont sat quietly reading his paper. He had witnessed too many of Miss Mary's outbreaks to be startled. Mrs. Bellmont interrogated Nig.

"I didn't do it! I didn't do it!" answered Nig, passionately, and then related the occurrence truthfully.

The discrepancy greatly enraged Mrs. Bellmont. With loud accusations and angry gestures she approached the child. Turning to her husband, she asked,

"Will you sit still, there, and hear that black nigger call Mary a liar?"

"How do we know that she has told the truth? I shall not punish her," he replied, and left the house, as he usually did when a tempest threatened to envelop him. No sooner was he out of sight than Mrs. B. and Mary commenced beating her inhumanly; then propping her mouth open with a piece of wood, shut her up in a dark room, without any supper. For employment, while the tempest raged within, Mr. Bellmont went for the cows, a task belonging to Frado, and thus unintentionally prolonged her pain. At dark Jack came in, and seeing Mary, accosted her with, "So you thought you'd vent your spite on Nig, did you? Why can't you let her alone? It was good enough for you to get a ducking, only you did not stay in half long enough."

"Stop!" said his mother. "You shall never talk so before me. You would have that little nigger trample on Mary, would you? She came home with a lie; it made Mary's story false."

"What was Mary's story?" asked Jack.

It was related.

"Now," said Jack, sallying into a chair, "the school-children happened to see it all, and they tell the same story Nig does. Which is most likely to be true, what a dozen agree they saw, or the contrary?"

"It is very strange you will believe what others say against your sister," retorted his mother, with a flashing eye. I think it is time your father subdued you."

"Father is a sensible man," argued Jack. "He would not wrong a dog. Where is Frado?" he continued.

"Mother gave her a good whipping and shut her up," replied Mary.

Just then Mr. Bellmont entered, and asked if Frado was "shut up yet."

The knowledge of her innocence, the perfidy of his sister, worked fearfully on Jack. He bounded from his chair, searched every room till he found the child; her mouth wedged apart, her face swollen, and full of pain.

How Jack pitied her! He relieved her jaws, brought her some supper, took her to her room, comforted her as well as he knew how, sat by her till she fell asleep, and then left for the sitting room. As he passed his mother, he remarked, "If that was the way Frado was to be treated, he hoped she would never wake again!" He then imparted her situation to his father, who seemed untouched, till a glance at Jack exposed a tearful eye. Jack went early to her next morning.

She awoke sad, but refreshed. After breakfast Jack took her with him to the field, and kept her through the day. But it could not be so generally. She must return to school, to her household duties. He resolved to do what he could to protect her from Mary and his mother. He bought her a dog, which became a great favourite with both. The invalid, Jane, would gladly befriend her; but she had not the strength to brave the iron will of her mother. Kind words and affectionate glances were the only expressions of sympathy she could safely indulge in. The men employed on the farm were always glad to hear Frado prattle; she was a great favourite with them. Mrs. Bellmont allowed them the privilege of talking with her in the kitchen. She did not fear that she should have ample opportunity of subduing her when they were away. Three months of schooling, summer and winter, she enjoyed for three years. Her winter overdress was a cast-off overcoat, once worn by Jack, and a sun-bonnet. It was a source of great merriment to the scholars, but Nig's retorts

were so mirthful, and their satisfaction so evident in attributing the
selection to "Old Granny Bellmont," that it was not painful to Nig or
pleasurable to Mary. Her jollity was not to be quenched by whipping
or scolding. In Mrs. Bellmont's presence she was under restraint; but
in the kitchen, and among her schoolmates, the pent-up fires burst
forth. She was ever at some sly prank when unseen by her teacher, in
school hours; not infrequently some outburst of merriment, of which
she was the original, was charged upon some innocent mate, and
punishment inflicted which she merited. They enjoyed her antics so
fully that any of them would suffer wrongfully to keep open the
avenues of mirth. She would venture far beyond propriety, thus
shielded and countenanced.

The teacher's desk was supplied with drawers, in which were
stored his books and other et ceteras of the profession. The children
observed Nig very busy there one morning before school, as they fitted in occasionally from their play outside. The master came; called
the children to order; opened a drawer to take the book the occasion
required; when out poured a volume of smoke. "Fire! fire!" screamed
he, at the top of his voice. By this time he had become sufficiently
acquainted with the peculiar odour, to know he was imposed upon.
The scholars shouted with laughter to see the terror of the dupe, who,
feeling abashed at the needless fright, made no very strict investiga-
tion, and Nig once more escaped punishment. She had provided herself with cigars, and puffing, puffing away at the crack of the drawer, had filled it with smoke, and then closed it tightly to deceive the
teacher, and amuse the scholars.

The interim of terms was filled up with a variety of duties new
and peculiar. At home, no matter how powerful the heat when sent
to rake hay or guard the grazing herd, she was never permitted to
shield her skin from the sun. She was not many shades darker than
Mary now; what a calamity it would be ever to hear the contrast spoken of. Mrs. Bellmont was determined the sun should have full
power to darken the shade which nature had first bestowed upon her
as best befitting.

WITH WHAT DIFFERING emotions have the denizens of earth
awaited the approach of today. Some sufferer has counted the vibrations of the pendulum impatient for its dawn, who, now that it has
arrived, is anxious for its close. The votary of pleasure, conscious of
yesterday's void, wishes for power to arrest time's haste till a few

more hours of mirth shall be enjoyed. The unfortunate are yet gazing in vain for golden-edged clouds they fancied would appear in their horizon. The good man feels that he has accomplished too little for the Master, and sighs that another day must so soon close. Innocent childhood, weary of its stay, longs for another morrow; busy childhood cries, hold! hold! and pursues it to another dawn. All are dissatisfied. All crave some good not yet possessed, which time is expected to bring with all its morrows.

Was it strange that, to a disconsolate child, three years should seem a long, long time? During school time she had rest from Mrs. Bellmont's tyranny. She was now nine years old; time, her mistress said, such privileges should cease.

She could now read and spell, and knew the elementary steps in grammar, arithmetic, and writing. Her education completed, as she said, Mrs. Bellmont felt that her time and person belonged solely to her. She was under her in every sense of the word. What an opportunity to indulge her vixen nature! No matter what occurred to ruffle her, or from what source provocation came, real or fancied, a few blows on Nig seemed to relieve her of a portion of ill-will.

These were days when Fido was the entire confidant of Frado. She told him her griefs as though he were human; and he sat so still, and listened so attentively, she really believed he knew her sorrows. All the leisure moments she could gain were used in teaching him some feat of dog-agility, so that Jack pronounced him very knowing, and was truly gratified to know he had furnished her with a gift answering his intentions.

Fido was the constant attendant of Frado, when sent from the house on errands, going and returning with the cows, out in the fields, to the village. If ever she forgot her hardships it was in his company.

Spring was now retiring. James, one of the absent sons, was expected home on a visit. He had never seen the last acquisition to the family. Jack had written faithfully of all the merits of his coloured *protégé*, and hinted plainly that mother did not always treat her just right. Many were the preparations to make the visit pleasant, and as the day approached when he was to arrive, great exertions were made to cook the favourite viands, to prepare the choicest table-fare.

The morning of the arrival day was a busy one. Frado knew not who would be of so much importance; her feet were speeding hither and thither so unsparingly. Mrs. Bellmont seemed a trifle fatigued, and her shoes which had, early in the morning, a methodic squeak,

145

altered to an irregular, peevish snap.

"Get some little wood to make the fire burn," said Mrs. Bellmont, in a sharp tone. Frado obeyed, bringing the smallest she could find.

Mrs. Bellmont approached her, and, giving her a box on her ear, reiterated the command.

The first the child brought was the smallest to be found; of course, the second must be a trifle larger. She well knew it was, as she threw it into a box on the hearth. To Mrs. Bellmont it was a greater affront, as well as larger wood, so she "taught her" with the rawhide, and sent her the third time for a little wood."

Nig, weeping, knew not what to do. She had carried the smallest; none left would suit her mistress; of course further punishment awaited her; so she gathered up whatever came first, and threw it down on the hearth. As she expected, Mrs. Bellmont, enraged, approached her, and kicked her so forcibly as to throw her upon the floor. Before she could rise, another foiled the attempt, and then followed kick after kick in quick succession and power, till she reached the door. Mr. Bellmont and Aunt Abby, hearing the noise, rushed in, just in time to see the last of the performance. Nig jumped up, and rushed from the house, out of sight. Aunt Abby returned to her apartment, followed by John, who was muttering to himself.

"What were you saying?" asked Aunt Abby.

"I said I hoped the child never would come into the house again."

"What would become of her? You cannot mean that," continued his sister.

"I do mean it. The child does as much work as a woman ought to; and just see how she is kicked about!"

"Why do you have it so, John?" asked his sister.

"How am I to help it? Women rule the earth, and all in it."

"I think I should rule my own house, John,"—

"And live in hell meantime," added Mr. Bellmont.

John now sauntered out to the barn to await the quieting of the storm.

Aunt Abby had a glimpse of Nig as she passed out of the yard; but to arrest her, or show her that she would shelter her, in Mrs. Bellmont's presence, would only bring reserved wrath on her defenceless head. Her sister-in-law had great prejudices against her. One cause of the alienation was that she did not give her right in the homestead to John, and leave it forever; another was that she was a professor of religion, (so was Mrs. Bellmont;) but Nab, as she called her, did not live according to her profession; another, that she would sometimes give Nig cake and pie, which she was never allowed to have at home. Mary had often noticed and spoken of her inconsistencies.

The dinner hour passed. Frado had not appeared. Mrs. B. made no inquiry or search. Aunt Abby looked long, and found her concealed in an outbuilding. "Come into the house with me," implored Aunt Abby.

"I ain't going in any more," sobbed the child.

"What will you do?" asked Aunt Abby.

"I've got to stay out here and die. I ain't got no mother, no home. I wish I was dead."

"Poor thing," muttered Aunt Abby; and slyly providing her with some dinner, left her to her grief.

Jane went to confer with her Aunt about the affair; and learned from her the retreat. She would gladly have concealed her in her own chamber, and ministered to her wants; but she was dependent on Mary and her mother for care, and any displeasure caused by attention to Nig, was seriously felt.

Toward night the coach brought James. A time of general greeting, inquiries for absent members of the family, a visit to Aunt Abby's room, undoing a few delicacies for Jane, brought them to the tea hour.

"Where's Frado?" asked Mr. Bellmont, observing she was not in her usual place, behind her mistress' chair.

"I don't know, and I don't care. If she makes her appearance again, I'll take the skin from her body," replied his wife.

James, a fine looking young man, with a pleasant countenance, placid, and yet decidedly serious, yet not stern, looked up confounded. He was no stranger to his mother's nature; but years of absence had erased the occurrences once so familiar, and he asked, "Is this that pretty little Nig, Jack writes to me about, that you are so severe upon, mother?"

"I'll not leave much of her beauty to be seen, if she comes in sight; and now, John," said Mrs, B., turning to her husband, "you need not think you are going to learn her to treat me in this way; just see how saucy she was this morning. She shall learn her place."

Mr. Bellmont raised his calm, determined eye full upon her, and said, in a decisive manner: "You shall not strike, or scald, or skin her, as you call it, if she comes back again. Remember!" and he brought his hand down upon the table. "I have searched an hour for her now, and she is not to be found on the premises. Do *you* know where she is? Is she *your* prisoner?"

"No! I have just told you I did not know where she was. Nab has her hid somewhere, I suppose. Oh, dear ! I did not think it would come to this; that my own husband would treat me so." Then came fast flowing tears, which no one but Mary seemed to notice. Jane crept into Aunt Abby's room; Mr. Bellmont and James went out of doors, and Mary remained to condole with her parent.

"Do you know where Frado is?" asked Jane of her aunt.

"No," she replied. "I have hunted everywhere. She has left her first hiding place. I cannot think what has become of her. There comes Jack and Fido; perhaps he knows;" and she walked to a window near, where James and his father were conversing together.

The two brothers exchanged a hearty greeting, and then Mr. Bellmont told Jack to eat his supper; afterward he wished to send him away. He immediately went in. Accustomed to all the phases of indoor storms, from a whine to thunder and lightning, he saw at a glance marks of disturbance. He had been absent through the day, with the hired men.

"What's the fuss?" asked he, rushing into Aunt Abby's.

"Eat your supper," said Jane; "go home, Jack."

Back again through the dining-room, and out to his father.

"What's the fuss ?" again inquired he of his father.

"Eat your supper, Jack, and see if you can find Frado. She's not been seen since morning, and then she was kicked out of the house."

"I shan't eat my supper till I find her," said Jack, indignantly. "Come, James, and see the little creature mother treats so."

They started, calling, searching, coaxing, all their way along. No Frado. They returned to the house to consult. James and Jack declared they would not sleep till she was found.

Mrs. Bellmont attempted to dissuade them from the search. "It was a shame a little nigger should make so much trouble."

Just then Fido came running up, and Jack exclaimed, "Fido knows where she is, I'll bet."

"So I believe," said his father; "but we shall not be wiser unless we can outwit him. He will not do what his mistress forbids him."

"I know how to fix him," said Jack. Taking a plate from the table, which was still waiting, he called, "Fido! Fido! Frado wants some supper. Come!" Jack started, the dog followed, and soon capered on before, far, far into the fields, over walls and through fences, into a piece of swampy land. Jack followed close, and soon appeared to James, who was quite in the rear, coaxing and forcing Frado along with him.

A frail child, driven from shelter by the cruelty of his mother, was an object of interest to James. They persuaded her to go home with them, warmed her by the kitchen fire, gave her a good supper, and took her with them into the sitting-room.

"Take that nigger out of my sight," was Mrs. Bellmont's command, before they could be seated.

James led her into Aunt Abby's, where he knew they were welcome. They chatted awhile until Frado seemed cheerful; then James led her to her room, and waited until she retired.

"Are you glad I've come home?" asked James.

"Yes; if you won't let me be whipped tomorrow."

"You won't be whipped. You must try to be a good girl," counseled James.

"If I do, I get whipped" sobbed the child. "They won't believe what I say. Oh, I wish I had my mother back; then I should not be kicked and whipped so. Who made me so?"

"God" answered James.

"Did God make you?"

"Yes."

"Who made Aunt Abby?"

"God."

"Who made your mother?"

"God."

"Did the same God that made her make me?"

"Yes."

"Well, then, I don't like him."

"Why not?"

"Because he made her white, and me black. Why didn't he make us *both* white?"

"I don't know; try to go to sleep, and you will feel better in the morning," was all the reply he could make to her knotty queries. It was a long time before she fell asleep; and a number of days before James felt in a mood to visit and entertain old associates and friends.

JAMES' VISIT CONCLUDED. Frado had become greatly attached to him, and with sorrow she listened and joined in the farewells which preceded his exit. The remembrance of his kindness cheered her through many a weary month, and an occasional word to her in letters to Jack, were like "cold waters to a thirsty soul." Intelligence came that James would soon marry; Frado hoped he would, and remove her from such severe treatment as she was subject to. There had been additional burdens laid on her since his return. She must now milk the cows, she had then only to drive. Flocks of sheep had been added to the farm, which daily claimed a portion of her time. In the absence of the men, she must harness the horse for Mary and her mother to ride, go to mill, in short, do the work of a boy, could one be procured to endure the tirades of Mrs. Bellmont. She was first up in the morning, doing what she could towards breakfast. Occasionally, she would utter some funny thing for Jack's benefit, while she was waiting on the table, provoking a sharp look from his mother, or expulsion from the room.

On one such occasion, they found her on the roof of the barn. Some repairs having been necessary, a staging had been erected, and was not wholly removed. Availing herself of ladders, she was mounted in high glee on the top-most board. Mr. Bellmont called sternly for her to come down; poor Jane nearly fainted from fear. Mrs. B. and Mary did not care if she "broke her neck," while Jack and the men laughed at her fearlessness. Strange, one spark of playfulness could remain amid such constant toil; but her natural temperament was in a high degree mirthful, and the encouragement she received from Jack and the hired men, constantly nurtured the inclination. When she had none of the family around to be merry with, she would amuse herself with the animals. Among the sheep was a willful leader, who always persisted in being first served, and many times in his fury he had thrown down Nig, till, provoked, she resolved to punish him. The pasture in which the sheep grazed was bounded on three sides by a wide stream, which flowed on one side at the base of precipitous banks. The first spare moments at her command, she ran to the pasture with a dish in her hand, and mounting the highest point of land nearest the stream, called the flock to their mock repast. Mr. Bellmont, with his labourer's, were in sight, though unseen by Frado. They paused to see what she was about to do. Should she by any mishap lose her footing, she must roll into the stream, and, without aid, must drown. They thought of shouting; but they feared an unexpected salute might startle her, and thus ensure what they were anxious to prevent. They watched in breathless silence. The willful sheep came furiously leaping and bounding far in advance of the flock. Just as he leaped for the dish, she suddenly jumped one side, when down he rolled into the river, and swimming across, remained alone till night. The men lay down, convulsed with laughter at the trick, and guessed at once its object. Mr. Bellmont talked seriously to the child for exposing herself to such danger; but she hopped about on her toes, and with laughable grimaces replied, she knew she was quick enough to "give him a slide."

But to return. James married a Baltimorean lady of wealthy parentage, an indispensable requisite, his mother had always taught him. He did not marry her wealth, though; he loved her, sincerely. She was not unlike his sister Jane, who had a social, gentle, loving nature, rather *too* yielding, her brother thought. His Susan had a firmness which Jane needed to complete her character, but which her ill health may in a measure have failed to produce. Although an invalid, she was not excluded from society. Was it strange *she* should seem a desirable companion, a treasure as a wife?

Two young men seemed desirous of possessing her. One was a neighbour, Henry Reed, a tall, spare young man, with sandy hair, and blue, sinister eyes. He seemed to appreciate her wants, and watch with interest her improvement or decay. His kindness she received, and by it was almost won. Her mother wished her to encourage his attentions. She had counted the acres which were to be transmitted to an only son; she knew there was silver in the purse; she would not have Jane too sentimental.

The eagerness with which he amassed wealth, was repulsive to Jane; he did not spare his person or beasts in its pursuit. She felt that to such a man she should be considered an incumbrance; she doubted if he would desire her, if he did not know she would bring a handsome patrimony. Her mother, full in favour with the parents of Henry, commanded her to accept him. She engaged herself, yielding to her mother's wishes, because she had not strength to oppose them; and sometimes, when witness of her mother's and Mary's tyranny, she felt any change would be preferable, even such a one as this. She knew her husband should be the man of her own selecting, one she was conscious of preferring before all others. She could not say this of Henry.

In this dilemma, a visitor came to Aunt Abby's; one of her boy-favourites, George Means, from an adjoining State. Sensible, plain looking, agreeable, talented, he could not long be a stranger to any one who wished to know him. Jane was accustomed to sit much with Aunt Abby always; her presence now seemed necessary to assist in entertaining this youthful friend. Jane was more pleased with him each day, and silently wished Henry possessed more refinement, and the polished manners of George. She felt dissatisfied with her relation to him. His calls while George was there, brought their opposing qualities vividly before her and she found it disagreeable to force herself into those attentions belonging to him. She received him apparently only as a neighbour.

George returned home, and Jane endeavoured to stifle the rising of dissatisfaction, and had nearly succeeded, when a letter came which needed but one glance to assure her of its birthplace; and she retired for its perusal. Well was it for her that her mother's suspicion was not aroused, or her curiosity startled to inquire who it came from. After reading it, she glided into Aunt Abby's, and placed it in her hands, who was no stranger to Jane's trials.

George could not rest after his return, he wrote, until he had communicated to Jane the emotions her presence awakened, and his desire to love and possess her as his own. He begged to know if his affections were reciprocated, or could be; if she would permit him to write to her; if she was free from all obligation to another.

"What would mother say?" queried Jane, as she received the letter from her aunt.

"Not much to comfort you."

"Now, aunt, George is just such a man as I could really love, I think, from all I have seen of him; you know I never could say that of Henry"—

"Then don't marry him," interrupted Aunt Abby.

"Mother will make me."

"Your father won't."

"Well, aunt, what can I do? Would you answer the letter, or not?"

"Yes, answer it. Tell him your situation."

"I shall not tell him all my feelings."

Jane answered that she had enjoyed his company much; she had seen nothing offensive in his manner or appearance; that she was under no obligations which forbade her receiving letters from him as a friend and acquaintance. George was puzzled by the reply. He wrote to Aunt Abby, and from her learned all. He could not see Jane thus sacrificed, without making an effort to rescue her. Another visit followed. George heard Jane say she preferred *him*. He then conferred with Henry at his home. It was not a pleasant subject to talk upon. To be thus supplanted, was not to be thought of He would sacrifice everything but his inheritance to secure his betrothed.

"And so you are the cause of her late coldness towards me. Leave! I will talk no more about it; the business is settled between us; there it will remain," said Henry.

"Have you no wish to know the real state of Jane's affections towards you?" asked George.

"No! Go, I say! go!" and Henry opened the door for him to pass out.

He retired to Aunt Abby's. Henry soon followed, and presented his cause to Mrs. Bellmont.

Provoked, surprised, indignant, she summoned Jane to her presence, and after a lengthy tirade upon Nab, and her satanic influence, told her she could not break the bonds which held her to Henry; she should not. George Means was rightly named; he was, truly, mean enough; she knew his family of old; his father had four wives, and five times as many children.

"Go to your room, Miss Jane," she continued. "Don't let me know of your being in Nab's for one while."

The storm was now visible to all beholders. Mr. Bellmont sought Jane. She told him her objections to Henry; showed him George's letter; told her answer, the occasion of his visit. He bade her not make herself sick; he would see that she was not compelled to violate her free choice in so important a transaction. He then sought the two young men; told them he could not as a father see his child compelled to an uncongenial union; a free, voluntary choice was of such importance to one of her health. She must be left free to her own choice.

Jane sent Henry a letter of dismission; he her one of a legal bearing, in which he balanced his disappointment by a few hundreds.

To brave her mother's fury, nearly overcame her, but the consolations of a kind father and aunt cheered her on. After a suitable interval she was married to George, and removed to his home in Vermont. Thus another light disappeared from Nig's horizon. Another was soon to follow. Jack was anxious to try his skill in providing for his own support; so a situation as clerk in a store was procured in a Western city, and six months after Jane's departure, was Nig abandoned to the tender mercies of Mary and her mother. As if to remove the last vestige of earthly joy, Mrs. Bellmont sold the companion and pet of Frado, the dog Fido.

THE SORROW OF Frado was very great for her pet, and Mr. Bellmont by great exertion obtained it again, much to the relief of the child. To be thus deprived of all her sources of pleasure was a sure way to exalt their worth, and Fido became, in her estimation, a more valuable presence than the human beings who surrounded her.

James had now been married a number of years, and frequent

requests for a visit from the family were at last accepted, and Mrs. Bellmont made great preparations for a fall sojourn in Baltimore. Mary was installed housekeeper—in name merely, for Nig was the only moving power in the house. Although suffering from their joint severity, she felt safer than to be thrown wholly upon an ardent, passionate, unrestrained young lady, whom she always hated and felt it hard to be obliged to obey. The trial she must meet. Were Jack or Jane at home she would have some refuge; one only remained; good Aunt Abby was still in the house.

She saw the fast receding coach which conveyed her master and mistress with regret, and begged for one favour only, that James would send for her when they returned, a hope she had confidently cherished all these five years.

She was now able to do all the washing, ironing, baking, and the common *et cetera* of household duties, though but fourteen. Mary left all for her to do, though she affected great responsibility. She would show herself in the kitchen long enough to relieve herself of some command, better withheld; or insist upon some compliance to her wishes in some department which she was very imperfectly acquainted with, very much less than the person she was addressing; and so impetuous till her orders were obeyed, that to escape the turmoil, Nig would often go contrary to her own knowledge to gain a respite.

Nig was taken sick! What could be done. The work, certainly, but not by Miss Mary. So Nig would work while she could remain erect, then sink down upon the floor, or a chair, till she could rally for a fresh effort. Mary would look in upon her, chide her for her laziness, threaten to tell mother when she came home, and so forth.

"Nig!" screamed Mary, on one of her sickest days, "come here, and sweep these threads from the carpet." She attempted to drag her weary limbs along, using the broom as support. Impatient of delay, she called again, but with a different request. "Bring me some wood, you lazy jade, quick." Nig rested the broom against the wall, and started on the fresh behest.

Too long gone. Flushed with anger, she rose and greeted her with, "What are you gone so long, for? Bring it in quick, I say."

"I am coming as quick as I can," she replied, entering the door.

"Saucy, impudent nigger, you! is this the way you answer me?" and taking a large carving knife from the table, she hurled it, in her rage, at the defenceless girl.

Dodging quickly, it fastened in the ceiling a few inches from

154

where she stood. There rushed on Mary's mental vision a picture of bloodshed, in which she was the perpetrator, and the sad consequences of what was so nearly an actual occurrence.

"Tell anybody of this, if you dare. If you tell Aunt Abby, I'll certainly kill you," said she, terrified. She returned to her room, brushed her threads herself; was for a day or two more guarded, and so escaped deserved and merited penalty.

Oh, how long the weeks seemed which held Nig in subjection to Mary; but they passed like all earth's sorrows and joys. Mr. and Mrs. B. returned delighted with their visit, and laden with rich presents for Mary. No word of hope for Nig. James was quite unwell, and would come home the next spring for a visit.

This, thought Nig, will be my time of release. I shall go back with him.

From early dawn until after all were retired, was she toiling, overworked, disheartened, longing for relief.

Exposure from heat to cold, or the reverse, often destroyed her health for short intervals. She wore no shoes until after frost, and snow even, appeared; and bared her feet again before the last vestige of winter disappeared. These sudden changes she was so ill guarded against, nearly conquered her physical system. Any word of complaint was severely repulsed or cruelly punished.

She was told she had much more than she deserved. So that manual labour was not in reality her only burden; but such an incessant torrent of scolding and boxing and threatening, was enough to deter one of maturer years from remaining within sound of the strife.

It is impossible to give an impression of the manifest enjoyment of Mrs. B. in these kitchen scenes. It was her favourite exercise to enter the appartment noisily, vociferate orders, give a few sudden blows to quicken Nig's pace, then return to the sitting room with such a satisfied expression, congratulating herself upon her thorough housekeeping qualities.

She usually rose in the morning at the ringing of the bell for breakfast; if she were heard stirring before that time, Nig knew well there was an extra amount of scolding to be borne.

No one now stood between herself and Frado, but Aunt Abby. And if she *dared* to interfere in the least, she was ordered back to her "own quarters." Nig would creep slyly into her room, learn what she could of her regarding the absent, and thus gain some light in the thick gloom of care and toil and sorrow in which she was immersed.

The first of spring a letter came from James, announcing declining health. He must try northern air as a restorative; so Frado joyfully prepared for this agreeable increase of the family, this addition to her cares.

He arrived feeble, lame, from his disease, so changed Frado wept at his appearance, fearing he would be removed from her forever. He kindly greeted her, took her to the parlour to see his wife and child, and said many things to kindle smiles on her sad face.

Frado felt so happy in his presence, so safe from maltreatment! He was to her a shelter. He observed, silently, the ways of the house a few days; Nig still took her meals in the same manner as formerly, having the same allowance of food. He, one day, bade her not remove the food, but sit down to the table and eat.

"She *will*, mother," said he, calmly, but imperatively; I'm determined; she works hard; I've watched her. Now, while I stay, she is going to sit down *here*, and eat such food as we eat."

A few sparks from the mother's black eyes were the only reply; she feared to oppose where she knew she could not prevail. So Nig's standing attitude, and selected diet vanished.

Her clothing was yet poor and scanty; she was not blessed with a Sunday attire; for she was never permitted to attend church with her mistress. "Religion was not meant for niggers," she said; when the husband and brothers were absent, she would drive Mrs. B. and Mary there, then return, and go for them at the close of the service, but never remain. Aunt Abby would take her to evening meetings, held in the neighbourhood, which Mrs. B. never attended; and impart to her lessons of truth and grace as they walked to the place of prayer.

Many of less piety would scorn to present so doleful a figure; Mrs. B. had shaved her glossy ringlets; and, in her coarse cloth gown and an ancient bonnet, she was anything but an enticing object. But Aunt Abby looked within. She saw a soul to save, an immortality of happiness to secure.

These evenings were eagerly anticipated by Nig; it was such a pleasant release from labour.

Such perfect contrast in the melody and prayers of these good people to the harsh tones which fell on her ears during the day.

Soon she had all their sacred songs at command, and enlivened her toil by accompanying it with this melody.

James encouraged his aunt in her efforts. He had found the Saviour, he wished to have Frado's desolate heart gladdened, quieted, sustained, by *His* presence. He felt sure there were elements in her heart which, transformed and purified by the gospel, would make

156

her worthy the esteem and friendship of the world. A kind, affectionate heart, native wit, and common sense, and the pertness she sometimes exhibited, he felt if restrained properly, might become useful in originating a self-reliance which would be of service to her in after years.

Yet it was not possible to compass all this, while she remained where she was. He wished to be cautious about pressing too closely her claims on his mother, as it would increase the burdened one he so anxiously wished to relieve. He cheered her on with the hope of returning with his family, when he recovered sufficiently. Nig seemed awakened to new hopes as aspirations, and realised a longing for the future, hitherto unknown. To complete Nig's enjoyment, Jack arrived unexpectedly. His greeting was as hearty to herself as to any of the family.

"Where are your curls, Fra?" asked Jack, after the usual salutation.

"Your mother cut them off."

"Thought you were getting handsome, did she? Same old story, is it; knocks and bumps? Better times coming; never fear, Nig."

How different this appellative sounded from him; he said it in such a tone, with such a roguish look!

She laughed, and replied that he had better take her West for a housekeeper.

Jack was pleased with James' innovations of table discipline, and would often tarry in the dining-room, to see Nig in her new place at the family table. As he was thus sitting one day, after the family had finished dinner, Frado seated herself in her mistress' chair, and was just reaching for a clean dessert plate which was on the table, when her mistress entered.

"Put that plate down; you shall not have a clean one; eat from mine," continued she. Nig hesitated. To eat after James, his wife or Jack, would have been pleasant; but to be commanded to do what was disagreeable by her mistress, because it was disagreeable, was trying. Quickly looking about, she took the plate, called Fido to wash it, which he did to the best of his ability; then, wiping her knife and fork on the cloth, she proceeded to eat her dinner.

Nig never looked toward her mistress during the process She had Jack near; she did not fear her now.

Insulted, full of rage, Mrs. Bellmont rushed to her husband, and commanded him to notice this insult; to whip that child; if he would not do it, James ought.

James came to hear the kitchen version of the affair. Jack was boiling over with laughter. He related all the circumstances to James, and pulling a bright, silver half-dollar from his pocket, he threw it at Nig, saying, "There, take that; 't was worth paying for."

James sought his mother; told her he "would not excuse or palliate Nig's impudence; but she should not be whipped or be punished at all. You have not treated her, mother, so as to gain her love; she is only exhibiting your remissness in this matter."

She only smothered her resentment until a convenient opportunity offered. The first time she was left alone with Nig, she gave her a thorough beating, to bring up arrearages; and threatened, if she ever exposed her to James, she would "cut her tongue out."

James found her, upon his return, sobbing; but fearful of revenge, she dared not answer his queries. He guessed their cause, and longed for returning health to take her under his protection.

JAMES DID NOT improve as was hoped. Month after month passed away, and brought no prospect of returning health. He could not walk far from the house for want of strength; but he loved to sit with Aunt Abby in her quiet room, talking of unseen glories, and heart-experiences, while planning for the spiritual benefit of those around them. In these confidential interviews, Frado was never omitted. They would discuss the prevalent opinion of the public, that people of colour are really inferior; incapable of cultivation and refinement. They would glance at the qualities of Nig, which promised so much if rightly directed. "I wish you would take her, James, when you are well, home with you," said Aunt Abby, in one of these seasons.

"Just what I am longing to do, Aunt Abby. Susan is just of my mind, and we intend to take her; I have been wishing to do so for years."

"She seems much affected by what she hears at the evening meetings, and asks me many questions on serious things; seems to love to read the Bible; I feel hopes of her."

"I hope she is thoughtful; no one has a kinder heart, one capable of loving more devotedly. But to think how prejudiced the world are towards her people; that she must be reared in such ignorance as to drown all the finer feelings. When I think of what she might be, of what she will be, I feel like grasping time till opinions change, and thousands like her rise into a noble freedom. I have seen Frado's grief, because she is black, amount to agony. It makes me sick to recall

158

these scenes. Mother pretends to think she don't know enough to sorrow for anything; but if she could see her as I have, when she supposed herself entirely alone, except her little dog Fido, lamenting her loneliness and complexion, I think, if she is not past feeling, she would retract. In the summer I was walking near the barn, and as I stood I heard sobs. 'Oh! oh!' I heard, 'why was I made? why can't I die? Oh, what have I to live for? No one cares for me only to get my work. And I feel sick; who cares for that? Work as long as I can stand, and then fall down and lay there till I can get up. No mother, father, brother or sister to care for me, and then it is, You lazy nigger, lazy nigger—all because I am black! Oh, if I could die!'

"I stepped into the barn, where I could see her. She was crouched down by the hay with her faithful friend Fido, and as she ceased speaking, buried her face in her hands, and cried bitterly; then, patting Fido, she kissed him, saying, 'You love me, Fido, don't you? but we must go work in the field.' She started on her mission; I called her to me, and told her she need not go, the hay was doing well.

"She has such confidence in me that she will do just as I tell her; so we found a seat under a shady tree, and there I took the opportunity to combat the notions she seemed to entertain respecting the loneliness of her condition and want of sympathising friends. I assured her that mother's views were by no means general; that in our part of the country there were thousands upon thousands who favoured the elevation of her race, disapproving of oppression in all its forms; that she was not unpitied, friendless, and utterly despised; that she might hope for better things in the future. Having spoken these words of comfort, I rose with the resolution that if I recovered my health I would take her home with me, whether mother was willing or not."

"I don't know what your mother would do without her; still, I wish she was away."

Susan now came for her long absent husband, and they returned home to their room.

The month of November was one of great anxiety on James' account. He was rapidly wasting away.

A celebrated physician was called, and performed a surgical operation, as a last means. Should this fail, there was no hope. Of course he was confined wholly to his room, mostly to his bed. With all his bodily suffering, all his anxiety for his family, whom he might not live to protect, he did not forget Frado. He shielded her from many beatings, and every day imparted religious instructions. No one, but his wife, could move him so easily as Frado; so that in addition to her daily toil she was often deprived of her rest at night.

Yet she insisted on being called; she wished to show her love for one who had been such a friend to her. Her anxiety and grief increased as the probabilities of his recovery became doubtful.

Mrs. Bellmont found her weeping on his account, shut her up, and whipped her with the rawhide, adding an injunction never to be seen snivelling again because she had a little work to do. She was very careful never to shed tears on his account, in her presence, afterwards.

THE BROTHER ASSOCIATED with James in business, in Baltimore, was sent for to confer with one who might never be able to see him there.

James began to speak of life as closing; of heaven, as of a place in immediate prospect; of aspirations, which waited for fruition in glory. His brother, Lewis by name, was an especial favourite of sister Mary; more like her, in disposition and preferences than James or Jack.

He arrived as soon as possible after the request, and saw with regret the sure indications of fatality in his sick brother, and listened to his admonitions—admonitions to a Christian life— with tears, and uttered some promises of attention to the subject so dear to the heart of James.

How gladly he would have extended healing aid. But, alas! it was not in his power; so, after listening to his wishes and arrangements for his family and business, he decided to return home.

Anxious for company home, he persuaded his father and mother to permit Mary to attend him. She was not at all needed in the sick room; she did not choose to be useful in the kitchen, and then she was fully determined to go.

So all the trunks were assembled and crammed with the best selections from the wardrobe of herself and mother, where the last-mentioned articles could be appropriated.

"Nig was never so helpful before," Mary remarked, and wondered what had induced such a change in place of former sullenness.

Nig was looking further than the present, and congratulating herself upon some days of peace, for Mary never lost opportunity of informing her mother of Nig's delinquencies, were she otherwise ignorant.

Was it strange if she were officious, with such relief in prospect?

The parting from the sick brother was tearful and sad. James prayed in their presence for their renewal in holiness; and urged their immediate attention to eternal realities, and gained a promise that Susan and Charlie should share their kindest regards.

No sooner were they on their way, than Nig slyly crept round to Aunt Abby's room, and tiptoeing and twisting herself into all shapes, she exclaimed,—

"She's gone, Aunt Abby, she's gone, fairly gone;" and jumped up and down, till Aunt Abby feared she would attract the notice of her mistress by such demonstrations.

"Well, she's gone, gone, Aunt Abby. I hope she'll never come back again."

"No! no! Frado, that's wrong! you would be wishing her dead; that won't do."

"Well, I'll bet she'll never come back again; somehow, I feel as though she wouldn't."

"She is James' sister," remonstrated Aunt Abby.

"So is our cross sheep just as much, that I ducked in the river; I'd like to try my hand at curing her too."

"But you forget what our good minister told us last week, about doing good to those that hate us."

"Didn't I do good, Aunt Abby, when I washed and ironed and packed her old duds to get rid of her, and helped her pack her trunks, and run here and there for her?"

"Well, well, Frado; you must go finish your work, or your mistress will be after you, and remind you severely of Miss Mary, and some others beside."

Nig went as she was told, and her clear voice was heard as she went, singing in joyous notes the relief she felt at the removal of one of her tormentors.

Day by day the quiet of the sick man's room was increased. He was helpless and nervous; and often wished change of position, thereby hoping to gain momentary relief. The calls upon Frado were consequently more frequent, her nights less tranquil. Her health was impaired by lifting the sick man, and by drudgery in the kitchen. Her ill health she endeavoured to conceal from James, fearing he might have less repose if there should be a change of attendants; and Mrs. Bellmont, she well knew, would have no sympathy for her. She was at last so much reduced as to be unable to stand erect for any great length of time. She would sit at the table to wash her dishes; if she heard the well known step of her mistress, she would rise till she returned to her room, and then sink down for further rest. Of course she was longer than usual in completing the services assigned her. This was a subject of complaint to Mrs. Bellmont; and Frado endeavoured to throw off all appearance of sickness in her presence.

But it was increasing upon her, and she could no longer hide her indisposition. Her mistress entered one day, and finding her seated, commanded her to go to work. "I am sick," replied Frado, rising and walking slowly to her unfinished task, "and cannot stand long, I feel so bad."

Angry that she should venture a reply to her command, she suddenly inflicted a blow which lay the tottering girl prostrate on the floor. Excited by so much indulgence of a dangerous passion, she seemed left to unrestrained malice; and snatching a towel, stuffed the mouth of the sufferer, and beat her cruelly.

Frado hoped she would end her misery by whipping her to death. She bore it with the hope of a martyr, that her misery would soon close. Though her mouth was muffled, and the sounds much stifled, there was a sensible commotion, which James' quick ear detected.

"Call Frado to come here," he said faintly, "I have not seen her to-day."

Susan retired with the request to the kitchen, where it was evident some brutal scene had just been enacted.

Mrs. Bellmont replied that she had "some work to do just now; when that was done, she might come."

Susan's appearance confirmed her husband's fears, and he requested his father, who sat by the bedside, to go for her. This was a messenger, as James well knew, who could not be denied; and the girl entered the room, sobbing and faint with anguish.

James called her to him, and inquired the cause of her sorrow. She was afraid to expose the cruel author of her misery, lest she should provoke new attacks. But after much entreaty, she told him all, much which had escaped his watchful ear. Poor James shut his eyes in silence, as if pained to forgetfulness by the recital. Then turning to Susan, he asked her to take Charlie, and walk out; "she needed the fresh air," he said. "And say to mother I wish Frado to sit by me till you return. I think you are fading, from staying so long in this sick room." Mr. B. also left, and Frado was thus left alone with her friend. Aunt Abby came in to make her daily visit, and seeing the sick countenance of the attendant, took her home with her to administer some cordial. She soon returned, however, and James kept her with him the rest of the day; and a comfortable night's repose following, she was enabled to continue, as usual, her labours. James insisted on her attending religious meetings in the vicinity with Aunt Abby.

Frado, under the instructions of Aunt Abby and the minister, became a believer in a future existence—one of happiness or misery. Her doubt was, is there a heaven for the black? She knew there was one for James, and Aunt Abby, and all good white people; but was there any for blacks? She had listened attentively to all the minister said, and all Aunt Abby had told her; but then it was all for white people.

As James approached that blessed world, she felt a strong desire to follow, and be with one who was such a dear, kind friend to her.

While she was exercised with these desires and aspirations, she attended an evening meeting with Aunt Abby, and the good man urged all, young or old, to accept the offers of mercy, to receive a compassionate Jesus as their Saviour. "Come to Christ," he urged, "all, young or old, white or black, bond or free, come all to Christ for pardon; repent, believe."

This was the message she longed to hear; it seemed to be spoken for her. But he had told them to repent; "what was that?" she asked. She knew she was unfit for any heaven, made for whites or blacks. She would gladly repent, or do anything which would admit her to share the abode of James.

Her anxiety increased; her countenance bore marks of solicitude unseen before; and though she said nothing of her inward contest, they all observed a change.

James and Aunt Abby hoped it was the springing of good seed sown by the Spirit of God. Her tearful attention at the last meeting encouraged his aunt to hope that her mind was awakened, her conscience aroused. Aunt Abby noticed that she was particularly engaged in reading the Bible; and this strengthened her conviction that a heavenly Messenger was striving with her. The neighbours dropped in to inquire after the sick, and also if Frado was "serious?" They noticed she seemed very thoughtful and tearful at the meetings. Mrs. Reed was very inquisitive; but Mrs. Bellmont saw no appearance of change for the better. She did not feel responsible for her spiritual culture, and hardly believed she had a soul.

Nig was in truth suffering much; her feelings were very intense on any subject, when once aroused. She read her Bible carefully, and as often as an opportunity presented, which was when entirely secluded in her own apartment, or by Aunt Abby's side, who kindly directed her to Christ, and instructed her in the way of salvation.

Mrs. Bellmont found her one day quietly reading her Bible. Amazed and half crediting the reports of officious neighbours, she felt it was time to interfere. Here she was, reading and shedding tears over the Bible. She ordered her to put up the book, and go to work, and not be snivelling about the house, or stop to read again.

But there was one little spot seldom penetrated by her mistress' watchful eye: this was her room, uninviting and comfortless; but to herself a safe retreat. Here she would listen to the pleadings of a Saviour, and try to penetrate the veil of doubt and sin which clouded her soul, and long to cast off the fetters of sin, and rise to the communion of saints.

Mrs. Bellmont, as we before said, did not trouble herself about the future destiny of her servant. If she did what she desired for *her* benefit, it was all the responsibility she acknowledged. But she seemed to have great aversion to the notice Nig would attract should she become pious. How could she meet this case? She resolved to make her complaint to John. Strange, when she was always foiled in this direction, she should resort to him. It was time something was done; she had begun to read the Bible openly.

The night of this discovery, as they were retiring, Mrs. Bellmont introduced the conversation, by saying:

"I want your attention to what I am going to say. I have let Nig go out to evening meetings a few times, and, if you will believe it, I found her reading the Bible today, just as though she expected to turn pious nigger, and preach to white folks. So now you see what good comes of sending her to school. If she should get converted she would have to go to meeting: at least, as long as James lives. I wish he had not such queer notions about her. It seems to trouble him to know he must die and leave her. He says if he should get well he would take her home with him, or educate her here. Oh, how awful! What can the child mean? So careful, too, of her! He says we shall ruin her health making her work so hard, and sleep in such a place. O, John! do you think he is in his right mind?"

"Yes, *yes*; she is slender."

"Yes, *yes!*" she repeated sarcastically, "you know these niggers are just like black snakes; you *can't* kill them. If she wasn't tough she would have been killed long ago. There was never one of my girls could do half the work."

"Did they ever try?" interposed her husband. "I think she can do

164

more than all of them together."

"What a man!" said she, peevishly. "But I want to know what is going to be done with her about getting pious?"

"Let her do just as she has a mind to. If it is a comfort to her, let her enjoy the privilege of being good. I see no objection."

"I should think you were crazy, sure. Don't you know that every night she will want to go toting off to meeting? and Sundays, too? and you know we have a great deal of company Sundays, and she can't be spared."

"I thought you Christians held to going to church," remarked Mr. B.

"Yes, but who ever thought of having a nigger go, except to drive others there? Why, according to you and James, we should very soon have her in the parlour, as smart as our own girls. It's of no use talking to you or James. If you should go on as you would like, it would not be six months before she would be leaving me; and that won't do. Just think how much profit she was to us last summer. We had no work hired out; she did the work of two girls—"

"And got the whippings for two with it!" remarked Mr. Bellmont.

"I'll beat the money out of her, if I can't get her worth any other way," retorted Mrs. B. sharply. While this scene was passing, Frado was trying to utter the prayer of the publican, "God be merciful to me a sinner."

SPRING OPENED, AND James, instead of rallying, as was hoped, grew worse daily. Aunt Abby and Frado were the constant allies of Susan. Mrs. Bellmont dared not lift him. She was not "strong enough," she said.

It was very offensive to Mrs. B. to have Nab about James so much. She had thrown out many a hint to detain her from so often visiting the sick-room; but Aunt Abby was too well accustomed to her ways to mind them. After various unsuccessful efforts, she resorted to the following expedient. As she heard her cross the entry below, to ascend the stairs, she slipped out and held the latch of the door which led into the upper entry.

"James does not want to see you, or any one else," she said.

Aunt Abby hesitated, and returned slowly to her own room; wondering if it were really James' wish not to see her. She did not venture again that day, but still felt disturbed and anxious about him. She inquired of Frado, and learned that he was no worse. She asked her if James did not wish her to come and see him; what could it mean?

Quite late next morning, Susan came to see what had become of her aunt.

"Your mother said James did not wish to see me, and I was afraid I tired him."

"Why, aunt, that is a mistake, I know. What could mother mean?" asked Susan.

The next time she went to the sitting-room she asked her mother,—

"Why does not Aunt Abby visit James as she has done? Where is she?"

"At home. I hope that she will stay there," was the answer.

"I should think she would come in and see James," continued Susan.

"I told her he did want to see her, and to stay out. You need make no stir about it; remember:"she added, with one of her fiery glances.

Susan kept silence. It was a day or two before James spoke of her absence. The family were at dinner, and Frado was watching beside him. He inquired the cause of her absence, and she told him all. After the family returned he sent his wife for her. When she entered, he took her hand, and said, "Come to me often, Aunt. Come any time,— I am always glad to see you. I have but a little longer to be with you,—come often, Aunt. Now please help lift me up, and see if I can rest a little."

Frado was called in, and Susan and Mrs. B. all attempted; Mrs. B. was too weak; she did not feel able to lift so much. So the three succeeded in relieving the sufferer.

Frado returned to her work. Mrs. B. followed. Seizing Frado, she said she would "cure her of tale-bearing," and, placing the wedge of wood between her teeth, she beat her cruelly with the rawhide. Aunt Abby heard the blows, and came to see if she could hinder them.

Surprised at her sudden appearance, Mrs. B. suddenly stopped, but forbade her removing the wood till she gave her permission, and commanded Nab to go home.

She was thus tortured when Mr. Bellmont came in, and, making inquiries which she did not, because she could not, answer, approached her; and seeing her situation, quickly removed the instrument of torture, and sought his wife. Their conversation we will omit; suffice to say, a storm raged which required many days to exhaust its strength.

Frado was becoming seriously ill. She had no relish for food, and was constantly overworked, and then she had such solicitude about the future. She wished to pray for pardon. She did try to pray. Her mistress had told her it would "do no-good for her to attempt prayer; prayer was for whites, not for blacks. If she minded her mistress, and did what she commanded, it was all that was required of her.

This did not satisfy her, or appease her longings. She knew her instructions did not harmonise with those of the man of God or Aunt Abby's. She resolved to persevere. She said nothing on the subject, unless asked. It was evident to all her mind was deeply exercised. James longed to speak with her alone on the subject. An opportunity presented soon, while the- family were at tea. It was usual to summon Aunt Abby to keep company with her, as his death was expected hourly.

As she took her accustomed seat, he asked, "Are you afraid to stay with me alone, Frado?"

"No," she replied, and stepped to the window to conceal her emotion.

"Come here, and sit by me; I wish to talk with you."

She approached him, and, taking her hand, he remarked:

"How poor you are, Frado! I want to tell you that I fear I shall never be able to talk with you again. It is the last time, perhaps, I shall ever talk with you. You are old enough to remember my dying words and profit by them. I have been sick a long time; I shall die pretty soon. My Heavenly Father is calling me home. Had it been his will to let me live I should take you to live with me; but, as it is, I shall go and leave you. But, Frado, if you will be a good girl, and love and serve God, it will be but a short time before we are in a heavenly home together. There will never be any sickness or sorrow there."

Frado, overcome with grief, sobbed, and buried her face in his pillow. She expected he would die; but to hear him speak of his departure himself was unexpected.

"Bid me good bye, Frado."

She kissed him, and sank on her knees by his bedside; his hand rested on her head; his eyes were closed; his lips moved in prayer for this disconsolate child.

His wife entered, and interpreting the scene, gave him some restoratives, and withdrew for a short time.

It was a great effort for Frado to cease sobbing; but she dared not be seen below in tears; so she choked her grief, and descended to her usual toil. Susan perceived a change in her husband. She felt that death was near.

He tenderly looked on her, and said, "Susan, my wife, our farewells are all spoken. I feel prepared to go. I shall meet you in heaven. Death is indeed creeping fast upon me. Let me see them all once more. Teach Charlie the way to heaven; lead him up as you come."

The family all assembled. He could not talk as he wished to them. He seemed to sink into unconsciousness. They watched him for hours. He had laboured hard for breath some time, when he seemed to awake suddenly, and exclaimed, "Hark! do you hear it?"

"Hear what, my son?" asked the father.

"Their call. Look, look, at the shining ones! Oh, let me go and be at rest!"

As if waiting for this petition, the Angel of Death severed the golden thread, and he was in heaven. At midnight the messenger came.

They called Frado to see his last struggle. Sinking on her knees at the foot of his bed, she buried her face in the clothes, and wept like one inconsolable. They led her from the room. She seemed to be too much absorbed to know it was necessary for her to leave. Next day she would steal into the chamber as often as she could, to weep over his remains, and ponder his last words to her. She moved about the house like an automaton. Every duty performed—but an abstraction from all, which showed her thoughts were busied elsewhere. Susan wished her to attend his burial as one of the family. Lewis and Mary and Jack it was not thought best to send for, as the season would not allow them time for the journey. Susan provided her with a dress for the occasion, which was her first intimation that she would be allowed to mingle her grief with others.

The day of the burial she was attired in her mourning dress; but Susan, in her grief, had forgotten a bonnet.

She hastily ransacked the closets, and found one of Mary's, trimmed with bright pink ribbon.

It was too late to change the ribbon, and she was unwilling to leave Frado at home; she knew it would be the wish of James she should go with her. So tying it on, she said, "Never mind, Frado, you shall see where our dear James is buried." As she passed out, she heard the whispers of the bystanders, "Look there! see there! how that looks,—a black dress and a pink ribbon!"

Another time, such remarks would have wounded Frado. She had now a sorrow with which such were small in comparison.

As she saw his body lowered in the grave she wished to share it;

but she was not fit to die. She could not go where he was if she did. She did not love God; she did not serve him or know how to.

She retired at night to mourn over her unfitness for heaven, and gaze out upon the stars, which, she felt, studded the entrance of heaven, above which James reposed in the bosom of Jesus, to which her desires were hastening. She wished she could see God, and ask him for eternal life. Aunt Abby had taught her that He was ever looking upon her. Oh, if she could see him, or hear him speak words of forgiveness. Her anxiety increased; her health seemed impaired, and she felt constrained to go to Aunt Abby and tell her all about her conflicts.

She received her like a returning wanderer; seriously urged her to accept of Christ; explained the way; read to her from the Bible, and remarked upon such passages as applied to her state. She warned her against stifling that voice which was calling her to heaven; echoed the farewell words of James, and told her to come to her with her difficulties, and not to delay a duty so important as attention to the truths of religion, and her soul's interests.

Mrs. Bellmont would occasionally give instruction, though far different. She would tell her she could not go where James was; she need not try. If she should get to heaven at all, she would never be as high up as he.

He was the attraction. Should she "want to go there if she could not see him?"

Mrs. B. seldom mentioned her bereavement, unless in such allusion to Frado. She donned her weeds from custom; kept close her crape veil for so many Sabbaths, and abated nothing of her characteristic harshness.

The clergyman called to minister consolation to the afflicted widow and mother. Aunt Abby seeing him approach the dwelling, knew at once the object of his visit, and followed him to the parlour, unasked by Mrs.B! What a daring affront! The good man dispensed the consolations, of which he was steward, to the apparently grief-smitten mother, who talked like one schooled in a heavenly atmosphere. Such resignation expressed, as might have graced the trial of the holiest. Susan, like a mute sufferer, bared her soul to his sympathy and godly counsel, but only replied to his questions in short syllables. When he offered prayer, Frado stole to the door that she might hear of the heavenly bliss of one who was her friend on earth. The prayer caused profuse weeping, as any tender reminder of the heaven-born was sure to. When the good man's voice ceased, she returned to her toil, carefully removing all trace of sorrow. Her mistress soon followed, irritated by Nab's impudence in presenting herself unasked in the parlour, and upraided her with indolence, and bade her apply herself more diligently. Stung by unmerited rebuke, weak from sorrow and anxiety, the tears rolled down her dark face, soon followed by sobs, and then losing all control of herself, she wept aloud. This was an act of disobedience. Her mistress grasping her rawhide, caused a longer flow of tears, and wounded a spirit that was craving healing mercies.

THE FAMILY, GATHERED by James' decease, returned to their homes. Susan and Charles returned to Baltimore. Letters were received from the absent, expressing their sympathy and grief. The father bowed like a "bruised reed," under the loss of his beloved son. He felt desirous to die the death of the righteous; also, conscious that he was unprepared, he resolved to start on the narrow way, and some time solicit entrance through the gate which leads to the celestial city. He acknowledged his too ready acquiescence with Mrs. B., in permitting Frado to be deprived of her only religious privileges for weeks together. He accordingly asked his sister to take her to meeting once more, which she was ready at once to do.

The first opportunity they once more attended meeting together. The minister conversed faithfully with every person present. He was surprised to find the little coloured girl so solicitous, and kindly directed her to the flowing fountain where she might wash and be clean. He inquired of the origin of her anxiety, of her progress up to this time, and endeavoured to make Christ, instead of James, the attraction of Heaven. He invited her to come to his house, to speak freely her mind to him, to pray much, to read her Bible often.

The neighbours, who were at meeting,— among them Mrs. Reed,—discussed the opinions Mrs. Bellmont would express on the subject. Mrs. Reed called and informed Mrs. B. that her coloured girl "related her experience the other night at the meeting."

"What experience?" asked she, quickly, as if she expected to hear the number of times she had whipped Frado, and the number of lashes set forth in plain Arabic numbers.

"Why, you know she is serious, don't you? She told the minister about it."

Mrs. B. made no reply, but changed the subject adroitly. Next morning she told Frado she "should not go out of the house for one while, except on errands; and if she did not stop trying to be religious, she would whip her to death."

Frado pondered; her mistress was a professor of religion; was she going to heaven? then she did not wish to go. If she should be near James, even, she could not be happy with those fiery eyes watching her ascending path. She resolved to give over all thought of the future world, and strove daily to put her anxiety far from her.

Mr. Bellmont found himself unable to do what James or Jack could accomplish for her. He talked with her seriously, told her he had seen her many times punished undeservedly; he did not wish to have her saucy or disrespectful, but when she was sure she did not deserve a whipping, to avoid it if she could. "You are looking sick," he added, "you cannot endure beating as you once could."

It was not long before an opportunity offered of profiting by his advice. She was sent for wood, and not returning as soon as Mrs. B. calculated, she followed her, and, snatching from the pile a stick, raised it over her.

"Stop!" shouted Frado, "strike me, and I'll never work a mite more for you;" and throwing down what she had gathered, stood like one who feels the stirring of free and independent thoughts.

By this unexpected demonstration, her mistress, in amazement, dropped her weapon, desisting from her purpose of chastisement. Frado walked towards the house, her mistress following with the wood she herself was sent after. She did not know, before, that she had a power to ward off assaults. Her triumph in seeing her enter the door with her burden, repaid her for much of her former suffering.

It was characteristic of Mrs. B. never to rise in her majesty, unless she was sure she should be victorious.

This affair never met with an "after clap," like many others.

Thus passed a year. The usual amount of scolding, but fewer whippings. Mrs. B. longed once more for Mary's return, who had been absent over a year; and she wrote imperatively for her to come quickly to her. A letter came in reply, announcing that she would comply as soon as she was sufficiently recovered from an illness which detained her.

No serious apprehensions were cherished by either parent, who constantly looked for notice of her arrival, by mail. Another letter brought tidings that Mary was seriously ill; her mother's presence was solicited.

She started without delay. Before she reached her destination, a letter came to the parents announcing her death.

No sooner was the astounding news received, than Frado rushed into Aunt Abby's, exclaiming:—

"She's dead, Aunt Abby!"

"Who?" she asked, terrified by the unprefaced announcement.

"Mary; they've just had a letter."

As Mrs. B. was away, the brother and sister could freely sympathise, and she sought him in this fresh sorrow, to communicate such solace as she could, and to learn particulars of Mary's untimely death, and assist him in his journey thither.

It seemed a thanksgiving to Frado. Every hour or two she would pop into Aunt Abby's room with some strange query:

"She got into the river again, Aunt Abby, didn't she; the Jordan is a big one to tumble into, any how. S'posen she goes to hell, she'll be as black as I am. Wouldn't mistress be mad to see her a nigger!" and others of a similar stamp, not at all acceptable to the pious, sympathetic dame; but she could not evade them.

The family returned from their sorrowful journey, leaving the dead behind. Nig looked for a change in her tyrant; what could subdue her, if the loss of her idol could not?

Never was Mrs. B. known to shed tears so profusely, as when she reiterated to one and another the sad particulars of her darling's sickness and death. There was, indeed, a season of quiet grief; it was the lull of the fiery elements. A few weeks revived the former tempests, and so at variance did they seem with chastisement sanctified, that Frado felt them to be able. She determined to flee. But where? Who would take her? Mrs. B. had always represented her ugly. Perhaps every one thought her so. Then no one would take her. She was black, no one would love her. She might have to return, and then she would be more in her mistress' power than ever.

She remembered her victory at the woodpile. She decided to remain to do as well as she could; to assert her rights when they were trampled on; to return once more to her meeting in the evening, which had been prohibited. She had learned how to conquer; she would not abuse the power while Mr. Bellmont was at home.

But had she not better run away? Where? She had never been from the place far enough to decide what course to take. She resolved to speak to Aunt Abby. She mapped the dangers of her course, her liability to fail in finding so good friends as John and herself. Frado's mind was busy for days and nights. She contemplated administering poison to her mistress, to rid herself and the house of so detestable a plague.

But she was restrained by an overruling Providence; and finally decided to stay contentedly through her period of service, which would expire when she was eighteen years of age.

In a few months Jane returned home with her family, to relieve her parents, upon whom years and affliction had left the marks of age. The years intervening since she had left her home, had, in some degree, softened the opposition to her unsanctioned marriage with George. The more Mrs. B. had about her, the more energetic seemed her directing capabilities, and her fault-finding propensities. Her own, she had full power over; and Jane after vain endeavours, became disgusted, weary, and perplexed, and decided that, though her mother might suffer, she could not endure her home. They followed Jack to the West. Thus vanished all hopes of sympathy or relief from this source to Frado. There seemed no one capable of enduring the oppressions of the house but her. She turned to the darkness of the future with the determination previously formed, to remain until she should be eighteen. Jane begged her to follow her so soon as she should be released; but so wearied out was she by her mistress, she felt disposed to flee from any and every one having her similitude of name or feature.

DARKNESS BEFORE DAY. Jane left, but Jack was now to come again. After Mary's death he visited home, leaving a wife behind. An orphan whose home was with a relative, gentle, loving, the true mate of kind, generous Jack. His mother was a stranger to her, of course, and had perfect right to interrogate:

"Is she good looking, Jack?" asked his mother.

"Looks well to me," was the laconic reply

"Was her father rich?"

"Not worth a copper, as I know of; I never asked him," answered Jack.

"Hadn't she any property? What did you marry her for," asked his mother.

"Oh, she's worth a million dollars, mother, though not a cent of it is in money."

"Jack! what do you want to bring such a poor being into the family, for? You'd better stay here, at home, and let your wife go. Why couldn't you try to do better, and not disgrace your parents?"

"Don't judge, till you see her," was Jack's reply, and immediately changed the subject. It was no recommendation to his mother, and she did not feel prepared to welcome her cordially now he was to come with his wife. He was indignant at his mother's advice to desert her. It rankled bitterly in his soul, the bare suggestion. He had more to bring. He now came with a child also. He decided to leave the West, but not his family.

Upon their arrival, Mrs. B. extended a cold welcome to her new daughter, eyeing her dress with closest scrutiny. Poverty was to her a disgrace, and she could not associate with any thus dishonoured. This coldness was felt by Jack's worthy wife, who only strove the harder to recommend herself by her obliging, winning ways.

Mrs. B. could never let Jack be with her alone without complaining of this or that deficiency in his wife.

He cared not so long as the complaints were piercing his own ears. He would not have Jenny disquieted. He passed his time in seeking employment.

A letter came from his brother Lewis, then at the South, soliciting his services. Leaving his wife, he repaired thither.

Mrs. B. felt that great restraint was removed, that Jenny was more in her own power. She wished to make her feel her inferiority; to relieve Jack of his burden if he would not do it himself She watched her incessantly, to catch at some act of Jenny's which might be construed into conjugal unfaithfulness.

Near by were a family of cousins, one a young man of Jack's age, who, from love to his cousin, proffered all needful courtesy to his stranger relative. Soon news reached Jack that Jenny was deserting her covenant vows, and had formed an illegal intimacy with his cousin. Meantime Jenny was told by her mother-in-law that Jack did not marry her untrammelled. He had another love whom he would be glad, even now, if he could, to marry. It was very doubtful if he ever came for her.

Jenny would feel pained by her unwelcome gossip, and, glancing at her child, she decided, however true it might be, she had a pledge which would enchain him yet. Ere long, the mother's inveterate hate crept out into some neighbour's enclosure, and, caught up hastily, they passed the secret round till it became none, and Lewis was sent for, the brother by whom Jack was employed. The neighbours saw her fade in health and spirits; they found letters never reached their destination when sent by either. Lewis arrived with the joyful news that he had come to take Jenny home with him.

What a relief to her to be freed from the gnawing taunts of her adversary.

Jenny retired to prepare for the journey, and Mrs. B. and Henry had a long interview. Next morning he informed Jenny that new clothes would be necessary, in order to make her presentable to Baltimore society, and he should return without her, and she must stay till she was suitably attired.

Disheartened, she rushed to her room, and, after relief from weeping, wrote to Jack to come; to have pity on her, and take her to him. No answer came. Mrs. Smith, a neighbour, watchful and friendly, suggested that she write away from home, and employ some one to carry it to the office who would elude Mrs. B., who, they very well knew, had intercepted Jenny's letter, and influenced Lewis to leave her behind. She accepted the offer, and Frado succeeded in managing the affair so that Jack soon came to the rescue, angry, wounded, and forever after alienated from his early home and his mother. Many times would Frado steal up into Jenny's room, when she knew she was tortured by her mistress' malignity, and tell some of her own encounters with her, and tell her she might "be sure it wouldn't kill her, for she should have died long before at the same treatment."

Susan and her child succeeded Jenny as visitors. Frado had merged into womanhood, and, retaining what she had learned, in spite of the few privileges enjoyed formerly, was striving to enrich her mind. Her school-books were her constant companions, and every leisure moment was applied to them. Susan was delighted to witness her progress, and some little book from her was a reward sufficient for any task imposed, however difficult. She had her book always fastened open near her, where she could glance from toil to soul refreshment. The approaching spring would close the term of years which Mrs. B. claimed as the period of her servitude. Often as she passed the waymarks of former years did she pause to ponder on her situation, and wonder if she could succeed in providing for her own wants. Her health was delicate, yet she resolved to try.

Soon she counted the time by days which should release her. Mrs. B. felt that she could not well spare one who could so well adapt herself to all departments—man, boy, housekeeper, domestic, etc. She begged Mrs. Smith to talk with her, to show her how ungrateful it would appear to leave a home of such comfort—how wicked it was to be ungrateful! But Frado replied that she had had enough of such comforts; she wanted some new ones; and as it was so wicked to be ungrateful, she would go from temptation; Aunt Abby said "we mustn't put ourselves in the way of temptation."

Poor little Fido! She shed more tears over him than over all beside.

The morning for departure dawned. Frado engaged to work for a family a mile distant. Mrs. Bellmont dismissed her with the assurance that she would soon wish herself back again, and a present of a silver half dollar.

Her wardrobe consisted of one decent dress, without any superfluous accompaniments. A Bible from Susan she felt was her greatest treasure.

Now was she alone in the world. The past year had been one of suffering resulting from a fall, which had left her lame.

The first summer passed pleasantly, and the wages earned were expended in garments necessary for health and cleanliness. Though feeble, she was well satisfied with her progress. Shut up in her room, after her toil was finished, she studied what poor samples of apparel she had, and, for the first time, prepared her own garments.

Mrs. Moore, who employed her, was a kind friend to her, and attempted to heal her wounded spirit by sympathy and advice, burying the past in the prospects of the future. But her failing health was a cloud no kindly human hand could dissipate. A little light work was all she could accomplish. A clergyman, whose family was small, sought her, and she was removed there. Her engagement with Mrs. Moore finished in the fall. Frado was anxious to keep up her reputation for efficiency, and often pressed far beyond prudence. In the winter she entirely gave up work, and confessed herself thoroughly sick. Mrs. Hale, soon overcome by additional cares, was taken sick also, and now it became necessary to adopt some measures for Frado's comfort, as well as to relieve Mrs. Hale. Such dark forebodings as visited her as she lay, solitary and sad, no moans or sighs could relieve.

The family physician pronounced her case one of doubtful issue. Frado hoped it was final. She could not feel relentings that her former home was abandoned, and yet, should she be in need of succour could she obtain it from one who would now so grudgingly bestow it? The family were applied to, and it was decided to take her there. She was removed to a room built out from the main building, used formerly as a workshop, where cold and rain found unobstructed access, and here she fought with bitter reminiscences and future prospects till she became reckless of her faith and hopes and person, and half wished to end what nature seemed so tardily to take.

Aunt Abby made her frequent visits, and at last had her removed to her own apartment, where she might supply her wants, and minister to her once more in heavenly things.

Then came the family consultation.

"What is to be done with her," asked Mrs. B., "after she is moved there with Nab?"

"Send for the Dr., your brother," Mr. B. replied.

"When?"

"To-night."

"To-night! and for her! Wait till morning," she continued.

"She has waited too long now; I think something should be done soon."

"I doubt if she is much sick," sharply interrupted Mrs. B.

"Well, we'll see what our brother thinks."

His coming was longed for by Frado, who had known him well during her long sojourn in the family; and his praise of her nice butter and cheese, from which his table was supplied, she knew he felt as well as spoke.

"You're sick, very sick," he said, quickly, after a moment's pause. "Take good care of her, Abby, or she'll never get well. All broken down."

"Yes, it was at Mrs. Moore's," said Mrs. B., "all this was done. She did but little the latter part of the time she was here."

"It was commenced longer ago than last summer. Take good care of her; she may never get well," remarked the Dr.

"We sha' n't pay you for doctoring her; you may look to the town for that, sir," said Mrs. B., and abruptly left the room.

"Oh dear! oh dear!" exclaimed Frado, and buried her face in the pillow.

A few kind words of consolation, and she was once more alone in the darkness which enveloped her previous days. Yet she felt sure they owed her a shelter and attention, when disabled, and she resolved to feel patient, and remain till she could help herself Mrs. B. would not attend her, nor permit her domestic to stay with her at all. Aunt Abby was her sole comforter. Aunt Abby's nursing had the desired effect, and she slowly improved. As soon as she was able to be moved, the kind Mrs. Moore took her to her home again, and completed what Aunt Abby had so well commenced. Not that she was well, or ever would be; but she had recovered so far as rendered it hopeful she might provide for her own wants. The clergyman at whose house she was taken sick, was now seeking some one to watch his sick children, and as soon as he heard of her recovery, again asked for her services.

What seemed so light and easy to others, was too much for Frado; and it became necessary to ask once more where the sick should find an asylum.

All felt that the place where her declining health began, should be the place of relief; so they applied once more for a shelter.

"No," exclaimed the indignant Mrs. B.; "she shall never come under this roof again; never! never!" she repeated, as if each repetition were a bolt to prevent admission.

One only resource; the public must pay the expense. So she was removed to the home of two maidens, (old,) who had principle enough to be willing to earn the money a charitable public disburses.

Three years of weary sickness wasted her, without extinguishing a life apparently so feeble. Two years had these maidens watched and cared for her, and they began to weary, and finally to request the authorities to remove her.

Mrs. Hoggs was a lover of gold and silver, and she asked the favour of filling her coffers by caring for the sick. The removal caused severe sickness.

By being bolstered in the bed, after a time she could use her hands, and often would ask for sewing to beguile the tedium. She had become very expert with her needle the first year of her release from Mrs. B., and she had forgotten none of her skill. Mrs. H. praised her, and as she improved in health, was anxious to employ her. She told her she could in this way replace her clothes, and as her board would be paid for, she would thus gain something.

Many times her hands wrought when body was in pain; but the hope that she might yet help herself, impelled her on.

Thus she reckoned her store of means by a few dollars, and was hoping soon to come in possession, when she was startled by the announcement that Mrs. Hoggs had reported her to the physician and town officers as an impostor. That she was, in truth, able to get up and go to work.

This brought on a severe sickness of two weeks, when Mrs. Moore again sought her, and took her to her home. She had formerly had wealth at her command, but misfortune had deprived her of it, and unlocked her heart to sympathies and favours she had never known while it lasted. Her husband, defrauded of his last means by a branch of the Bellmont family, had supported them by manual labour, gone to the West, and left his wife and four young children. But she felt humanity required her to give a shelter to one she knew to be worthy of a hospitable reception. Mrs. Moore's physician was called, and pronounced her a very sick girl, and encouraged Mrs. M. to keep her and care for her, and he would see that the authorities were informed of Frado's helplessness, and pledged assistance.

Here she remained till sufficiently restored to sew again. Then came the old resolution to take care of herself, to cast off the unpleasant charities of the public.

She learned that in some towns in Massachusetts, girls make straw bonnets—that it was easy and profitable. But how should she, black, feeble and poor, find any one to teach her. But God prepares the way, when human agencies see no path. Here was found a plain, poor, simple woman, who could see merit beneath a dark skin; and when the invalid mulatto told her sorrows, she opened her door and her heart, and took the stranger in. Expert with the needle, Frado soon equalled her instructress; and she sought also to teach her the value of useful books; and while one read aloud to the other of deeds historic and names renowned, Frado experienced a new impulse. She felt herself capable of elevation; she felt that this book information supplied an undefined dissatisfaction she had long felt, but could not express. Every leisure moment was carefully applied to self-improvement and a devout and Christian exterior invited confidence from the villagers. Thus she passed months of quiet, growing in the confidence of her neighbours and new found friends.

A FEW YEARS ago, within the compass of my narrative, there appeared often in some of our New England villages, professed fugitives from slavery, who recounted their personal experience in homely phrase, and awakened the indignation of non-slaveholders against brother Pro. Such a one appeared in the new home of Frado; and as people of colour were rare there, was it strange she should attract her dark brother; that he should inquire her out; succeed in seeing her; feel a strange sensation in his heart towards her; that he should toy with her shining curls, feel proud to provoke her to smile and expose the ivory concealed by thin, ruby lips; that her sparkling eyes should fascinate; that he should propose; that they should marry? A short acquaintance was indeed an objection, but she saw him often, and thought she knew him. He never spoke of his enslavement to her when alone, but she felt that, like her own oppression, it was painful to disturb oftener than was needful.

He was a fine, straight negro, whose back showed no marks of the lash, erect as if it never crouched beneath a burden. There was a silent sympathy which Frado felt attracted her, and she opened her heart to the presence of love— that arbitrary and inexorable tyrant.

She removed to Singleton, her former residence, and there was married. Here were Frado's first feelings of trust and repose on human arm. She realised, for the first time, the relief of looking to another for comfortable support. Occasionally he would leave her to "lecture."

Those tours were prolonged often to weeks. Of course he had little spare money. Frado was again feeling her self-dependence, and was at last compelled to resort alone to that. Samuel was kind to her when at home, but made no provision for his absence, which was at last unprecedented.

He left her to her fate—embarked at sea, with the disclosure that he had never seen the South, and that his illiterate harangues were humbugs for hungry abolitionists. Once more alone! Yet not alone. A still newer companionship would soon force itself upon her. No one wanted her with such prospects. Herself was burden enough; who would have an additional one?

The horrors of her condition nearly prostrated her, and she was again thrown upon the public for sustenance. Then followed the birth of her child. The long absent Samuel unexpectedly returned, and rescued her from charity. Recovering from her expected illness, she once more commenced toil for herself and child, in a room obtained of a poor woman, but with better fortune. One so well known would not be wholly neglected. Kind friends watched her when Samuel was from home, prevented her from suffering, and when the cold weather pinched the warmly clad, a kind friend took them in, and thus preserved them. At last Samuel's business became very engrossing, and after long desertion, news reached his family that he had become a victim of yellow fever, in New Orleans.

So much toil as was necessary to sustain Frado, was more than she could endure. As soon as her babe could be nourished without his mother, she left him in charge of a Mrs. Capon, and procured an agency, hoping to recruit her health, and gain an easier livelihood for herself and child. This afforded her better maintenance than she had yet found. She passed into the various towns of the State she lived in, then into Massachusetts. Strange were some of her adventures. Watched by kidnappers, maltreated by professed abolitionists, who didn't want slaves at the South, nor niggers in their own houses, North. Faugh! to lodge one; to eat with one; to admit one through the front door; to sit next one; awful!

Traps slyly laid by the vicious to ensnare her, she resolutely avoided. In one of her tours, Providence favoured her with a friend who, pitying her cheerless lot, kindly provided her with a valuable recipe, from which she might herself manufacture a useful article for her maintenance. This proved a more agreeable, and an easier way of sustenance.

And thus, to the present time, may you see her busily employed in preparing her merchandise; then sallying forth to encounter many frowns, but some kind friends and purchasers. Nothing turns her from her steadfast purpose of elevating herself. Reposing on God, she has thus far journeyed securely. Still an invalid, she asks your sympathy, gentle reader. Refuse not, because some part of her history is unknown, save by the Omniscient God. Enough has been unrolled to demand your sympathy and aid.

Do you ask the destiny of those connected with her early history? A few years only have elapsed since Mr. and Mrs. B. passed into another world. As age increased, Mrs. B. became more irritable, so that no one, even her own children, could remain with her; and she was accompanied by her husband to the home of Lewis, where, after an agony in death unspeakable, she passed away. Only a few months since, Aunt Abby entered heaven. Jack and his wife rest in heaven, disturbed by no intruders; and Susan and her child are yet with the living. Jane has silver locks in place of auburn tresses, but she has the early love of Henry still, and has never regretted her exchange of lovers. Frado has passed from their memories, as Joseph from the butler's, but she will never cease to track them till beyond mortal vision.

Books with ATTITUDE

WIN £1,000 AND GET YOUR NOVEL PUBLISHED

You have a novel inside your head. We want to publish it. Send for details of the UK's biggest black book prize to: Xpress Yourself '97, 55 Broadway Market, London E8 4PH

CLOSING DATE: December 31st 1996